CHICAGO BY NIGHT

Frommer's

CHICAGO by Night

BY

TODD SAVAGE

A BALLIETT & FITZGERALD BOOK

MACMILLAN • USA

a disclaimer

Prices fluctuate in the course of time, and travel information changes under the impact of the varied and volatile factors that influence the travel industry. Neither the author nor the publisher can be held responsible for the experiences of readers while traveling. Readers are invited to write to the publisher with ideas, comments, and suggestions for future editions.

about the authors

Todd Savage is a freelance writer and researcher based in Chicago who has contributed to the *Irreverent Guide to Chicago,* as well as to *Chicago* magazine, the *Chicago Tribune, Chicago Reader, Town and Country,* and *Outside.*

Dan Santow, who contributed the Late Night Dining chapter, is the principal author of the *Irreverent Guide to Chicago.*

Balliett & Fitzgerald, Inc.
Executive editor: Tom Dyja
Managing editor: Duncan Bock
Associate editor: Howard Slatkin
Assistant editor: Maria Fernandez
Editorial assistants: Ruth Ro, Bindu Poulose, Donna Spillane, Catie O'Brien

Macmillan Travel art director: Michele Laseau

MACMILLAN TRAVEL
A Simon & Schuster Macmillan Company
1633 Broadway
New York, NY 10019

ISBN 0-02-861131-4
Library of Congress information available from Library of Congress.

special sales

Bulk purchases (10+ copies) of Frommer's and selected Macmillan travel guides are available to corporations, organizations, institutions, and charities at special discounts, and can be customized to suit individual needs. For more information write to Special Sales, Macmillan General Reference, 1633 Broadway, New York, NY 10019.

Manufactured in the United States of America

contents

Chicago Orientation

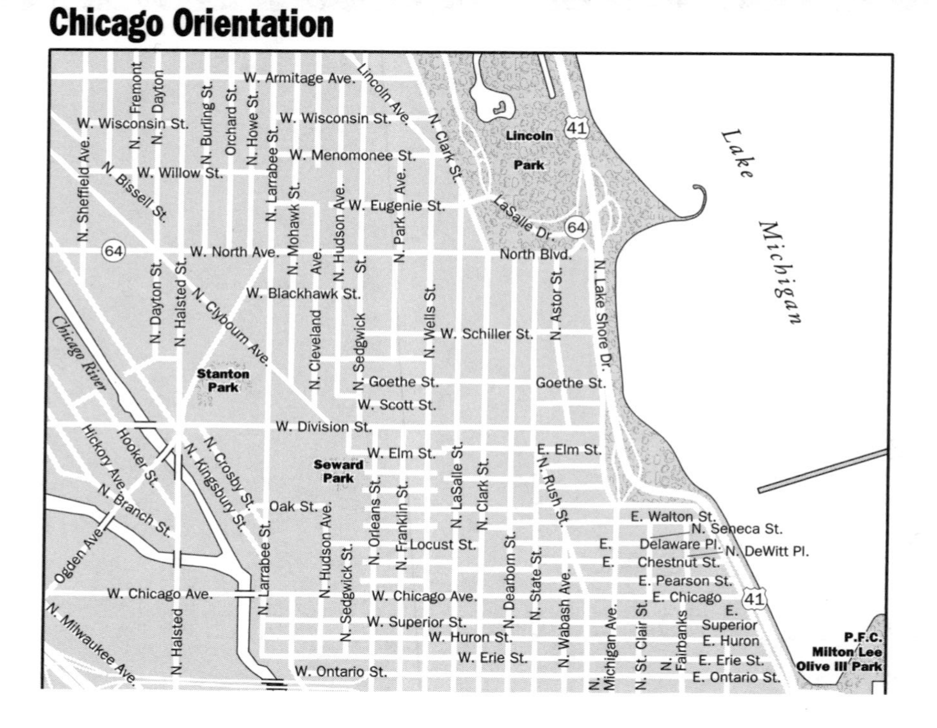

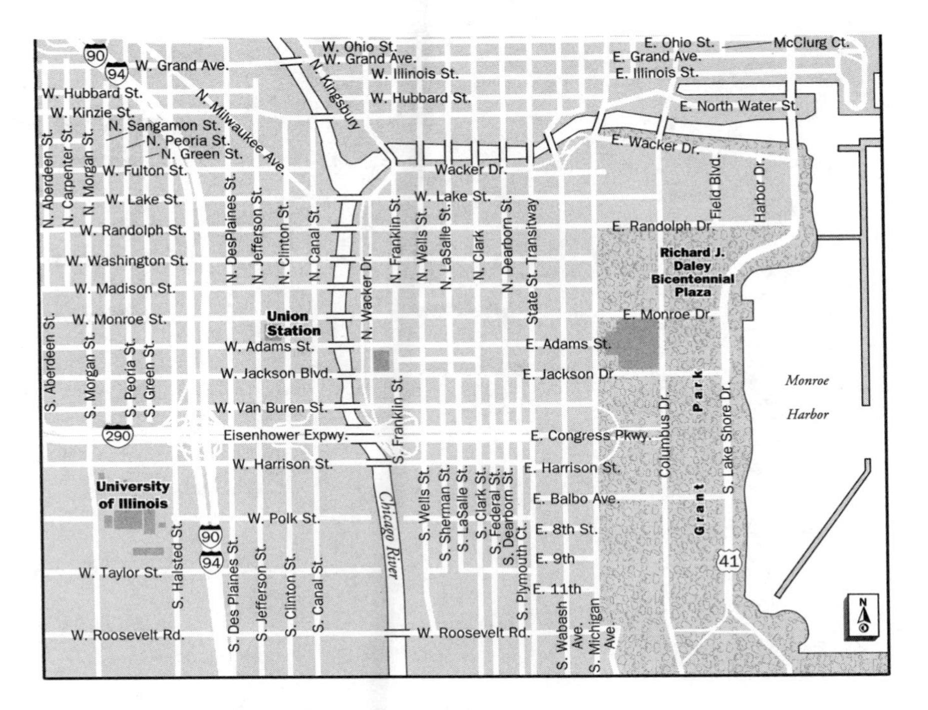

W. Ohio St.
W. Grand Ave.
W. Illinois St.
W. Hubbard St.
E. Ohio St.
McClurg Ct.
E. Grand Ave.
E. Illinois St.
E. North Water St.
E. Wacker Dr.
W. Grand Ave.
W. Hubbard St.
W. Kinzie St.
N. Sangamon St.
N. Peoria St.
N. Green St.
N. Milwaukee Ave.
N. Kingsbury
Wacker Dr.
W. Fulton St.
W. Lake St.
W. Randolph St.
W. Washington St.
W. Madison St.
W. Monroe St.
N. Aberdeen St.
N. Carpenter St.
N. Morgan St.
N. DesPlaines St.
N. Jefferson St.
N. Clinton St.
N. Canal St.
N. Wacker Dr.
N. Franklin St.
W. Lake St.
N. Wells St.
N. LaSalle St.
N. Clark
N. Dearborn St.
State St. Transitway
Field Blvd.
Harbor Dr.
E. Randolph Dr.
Richard J. Daley Bicentennial Plaza
E. Monroe Dr.
Union Station
W. Adams St.
W. Jackson Blvd.
W. Van Buren St.
Eisenhower Expwy.
W. Harrison St.
E. Adams St.
E. Jackson Dr.
E. Congress Pkwy.
E. Harrison St.
E. Balbo Ave.
E. 8th St.
E. 9th
E. 11th
Columbus Dr.
Grant Park
S. Lake Shore Dr.
Monroe Harbor
41
S. Aberdeen St.
S. Morgan St.
S. Peoria St.
S. Green St.
290
University of Illinois
W. Polk St.
S. Halsted St.
90
94
W. Taylor St.
W. Roosevelt Rd.
S. Des Plaines St.
S. Jefferson St.
S. Clinton St.
S. Canal St.
Chicago River
S. Franklin St.
S. Wells St.
S. Sherman St.
S. LaSalle St.
S. Clark St.
S. Federal St.
S. Dearborn St.
S. Plymouth Ct.
W. Roosevelt Rd.
S. Wabash Ave.
S. Michigan Ave.
N

what's hot, what's not

Chicago is a driving city—and we don't just mean the pace. People have cars here, and they use them, especially at night. If you want to get a sense of what this town's like after dark, get on one of its unbending streets like Halsted, downtown west of the Chicago River, and head north. The road keeps going—from the South Side it's 23 miles long, but let's just look at five miles. You'll pass a chic new restaurant enclave in the city's working produce market. Then comes the downtown gulch of huge, bland night clubs, a black gay disco pounding with house music, and a notorious housing project. Minutes later you cross into Lincoln Park and sight the city's most famous theater company. Then it's on to the long stretch of restaurants and bars with Irish names (but no real Irish people to speak of). Next, more pickup bars, blues bars, British pubs, and sports bars. Pulled-over cabs snarl the traffic, as laughing young preppy guys and gals spill out of them. Then, following the empty cabs, you cross Belmont, and here in the city's gay hometown the streets are just as crowded. Young men and some female couples are holding hands, sitting at windowside perches in bars, video bars, and cafes. Soon Halsted feeds like a tributary into Broadway, which continues its northward path….

Chicago is a city of neighborhoods, each with its own mood, fried chicken shacks giving way to stunning architecture in moments. Don't buy the placid Midwestern facade. In one of the Windy City's thriving and unique neighborhoods—whether it's Wicker Park or Hyde Park—you'll find something that suits your taste. You name it, 12-bar blues or stylish cabaret.

Best to you on your jag into the night.

What's hot

Dennis Rodmania... Both club kids and sports die hards are bullish on Rodman: the NBA bad boy's nocturnal haunts have become the bold-faced stuff of gossip columns. When he's not pulling down rebounds at the **United Center** (see Sports), Rodman may be making the scene at the megaclub **Crobar** (see The Club Scene) or parting the crowd with the bold and beautiful at **Adagio** (see The Bar Scene). He's given celebrity-deprived Chicagoans a whole new reason to go out at night: to see if he's there.

Retro... What's old is new again. Everybody's drinking martinis, and they're doing it at some slick new clubs and eateries dressed up in faux pre-War high style, from the gorgeous ballroom-size jazz club **Green Dolphin Street** to the hotel bar **Green Orchid Room** with its satin-skirted cocktail waitresses, and from the deluxe deco bowling alley-cum-bar **The Lucky Strike** to the swank forties-style Italian supper club **Club Lucky**. But for the genuine article, slip into a faded velvet booth at the **Green Mill**, an Uptown jazz club with a gangster pedigree that hasn't changed a thing since the thirties. The old upright cash register and rotary phone at the bar aren't props. (See The Club and Bar Scenes.)

Dining on the edge... Here's a guaranteed strategy for a hot restaurant in Chicago: Find some spooky warehouse district or down-at-its-heels working-class 'hood (the more broken malt liquor bottles on the sidewalk the better), hire a chef steeped in fusion cooking, and decorate. Spend a wad on sculptural light fixtures and faux paint finishes or pick up some kitschy cups at a thrift shop and a bunch of wobbly tables and chairs—it doesn't matter. Oh yeah, don't advertise. Chicagoans will drive around trying to find you; the thrill of the chase fuels their appetite. You're sure to be a hit, just like way-chic **Marché** in the Randolph Street market district and earthy slackateria **Bite** in Ukrainian Village. (See Late Night Dining.)

The play's the thing... No one's building skyscrapers in Chicago anymore; the construction racket you hear is the sound of the city's theater boom. Now a ghost town after dark, the North Loop may soon relive its heyday, when the sidewalks were filled with people going to shows. A refurbished Oriental Theatre off State Street is soon to open, a block from the Chicago Theatre and its new Disney tenants. The **Goodman Theatre**, the city's oldest resident theater, has been making noises about renovating a Selwyn and Harris theater. On the north side of the Chicago River, a new complex providing a permanent home for many of the city's smaller companies should begin rising soon. The small, handsome **Mercury Theater** on a blossoming restaurant and retail row in the arty Lake View neighborhood debuted in 1996. So what if a few of the city's mid-size stages have gone belly up in the last few years? A new generation of thespians carries on: In Chicago, neighborhood storefront companies are about as ubiquitous as hot dog stands. And many have night-owl performances geared to Gen X tastes and sleep cycles. (See The Arts.)

Wicker Park... Shorthand in Chicago for what's cool, or what's trying to be. As in, "Your new nose ring is so *Wicker Park.*" The artists who led the waves of gentrification in this Northwest Side neighborhood in the eighties are already looking for cheaper lofts, but it's still a slightly edgy haven for bohemian types and thrill-seeking job holders. Ground zero is the hurly-burly confluence of North, Damen, and Milwaukee avenues, where traffic crawls on weekends. Here, funky new restaurants with $20 entrees, alternative rock clubs, and galleries have made a truce with old Polish diners, discount furniture stores, and Spanish-speaking doctor's offices.

Museum cocktail hours... Those NEA cuts have been an unexpected boon to Chicago nightlife. Courting a new generation of youthful members, the **Art Institute of Chicago** was the first bastion of high culture to turn its galleries over to hordes of power-suited young professionals for a night of Monet and merlot. The Institute's wildly popular, monthly After Hours event (See Hanging Out) has inspired knock-offs everywhere from **Shedd Aquarium** to the Newberry Library. In the Institute's lobby, check out the junior ad execs wearing DKNY suits trying to stuff their coats in the coin-operated bag lockers so they can skip the backed-up check line. If you ever make it past the packed Grand Staircase, the art, of course, is splendid—with sightlines free of the usual daytime mobs.

The caffeine scene... Where were we hanging out a few years ago? Hard to imagine life before the coffehouse, especially since it fits so well with the terrain here. A walking, train-riding population needs pit stops. And now we've got them in spades. Few Chicago cafes capture the new esprit de corps better than **The Third Coast**, a Gold Coast see-and-be-seen spot, and **Urbis Orbis**, a lofted Wicker Park coffeehouse with a grungy, lived-in feel. (See The Bar Scene.)

Beer boutiques and microbrews... Chicago connoisseurs no longer have to settle for just the fruity taste of hometown standard Old Style. Every semi-sophisticated neighborhood bar seems to claim they've got the widest selection of beers in town. A few that come close: **Sheffield's Beer & Wine Garden** in Lake View, **Hopleaf** in Andersonville, and **House of Beer** in the thick of the Division Street singles area. (See The Bar Scene.)

What's not

Big dance clubs... Every day there seems to be fewer places for club kids to find work these days. Those clubs still standing haven't been hip for years. They're just too much work. All that fussing in front of the mirror. Parking. The inevitable, humiliating wait to fork over your ten bucks. When Chicagoans want to shake loose and break into a sweat, hassle-free, they're looking for intimate bars with dance floors tucked away—places like the hipster pad **Liar's Club** or the arty gay bar **Big Chicks**—that are fun and out of your face. (See The Club and Bar Scenes.)

Night games at Wrigley Field... Neighbors lost their fight against the behemoth Tribune Company and its Wrigley night lights years ago, but theirs was a moral victory. Going to a **Cubs** game after dark robs the park of much of its considerable daytime charm—particularly for those among us who like to skip out of work after a big lunch, sit in the right field bleachers with other slackers, hurl insults at those slobs in the left field bleachers (or vice versa), and squint in the afternoon sun while baking to a painful crisp. Tonight, go out to dinner, a club, whatever—catch the 1:20pm game tomorrow. (See Sports.)

Cigar bars... Let the backlash begin. Stogies have been lighting up all over town, giving puffed-up blowhards in flashy suits all the more reason to act even jerkier. In the beginning it was an amusing novelty and acceptable at a clubby restaurant like **Harry's Velvet Room**, where cigars are part of the retro-schtick, or in the smoking lounge at **Drink**, which has its own humidor. But nowadays cigars are showing up in every bar in town. Isn't it time to clear the air? Among the best cigar-free, even the totally smoke-free, hangouts are a couple of anomalous night spots: the comfy Wrigleyville coffeehouse **Uncommon Ground** and **Jazz Showcase**, an upscale River North music club where smoke won't get in your eyes. (See The Bar and Club Scenes.)

Rush Street... Shorthand for what's uncool in Chicago. As in, "That pick-up place is so *Rush Street.*" It's heyday is past: Though a few jazz lounges like long-timer **The Backroom** (see The Club Scene) distinguish it, the old strip has sobered up in the nineties with a mix of shops and swinging restaurants like **Gibsons Bar and Steakhouse** (see Late Night Dining). And to be fair, Rush Street is often used as a synonym for the real culprit: The block of nearly interchangeable meat-market bars on Division Street.

Buzz-killing bureaucrats... Da Mayor and his tight-fisted liquor license commissioner are not the life of the party in this town. In their bid to bring a peaceful, quiet... well, suburban, calm to the city, they've put a moratorium on new liquor licenses in areas of "undue concentration" (like Halsted), made it very hard and glacially slow to get licenses anywhere in town, and sent undercover underage agents into bars to buy drinks without proper identifaction. As a result, tavern owners guard their licenses for dear life, and card people old enough to be your grandfather.

the clu

1

b scene

Nobody will ever accuse the city's jazz and blues scenes of failing to pay dues. They're older than the hills, and despite slow periods, have never become quaint or nostalgic, thanks to periodic resurgences. Take jazz, for example. The drifting Chicago jazz circuit recently got a solid anchor when impresario Joe Segal opened fancy new digs for his Jazz Showcase. A new star was born when local boy Kurt Elling got signed to Blue Note Records after the label's president caught him at the Green Mill, one of the city's liveliest jazz spots. And among the old-timers, Barrett Deems, a rascally octogenarian drummer who trotted the globe with Louis Armstrong, still swings his 18-piece orchestra through the paces at clubs around town. Blues lovers have their pick of yuppie Lincoln Park spots or the South Side's funky old Checkerboard Lounge, one of the last of its kind on a strip where blues clubs once rocked. And even Buddy Guy, who has his own fine club, showed an altruistic blues-loving heart when he showed up at a press conference for a potential new competitor, the theme club House of Blues, which was planning its new downtown outlet in Chicago.

On the rock front, a few short years ago—a few Ice Ages ago in pop life—Chicago was fleetingly burdened with being called the next latest, greatest Seattle. The ascendant Smashing Pumpkins and Liz Phair were the biggest thing since, well, Cheap Trick. Wicker Park became the cradle of hip civilization in Chicago. All self-respecting rocker wannabes decided they just had to live in this pierced-and-tattooed 'hood. (After all, it was the only way to keep an eye on all those "drummer wanted" fliers.) With a blend of true Midwestern modesty and too-cool-for-school rocker indifference, the kids acted like they didn't care about outsider attention. Amusing maps appeared in *Billboard* magazine highlighting all the clubs and slacker coffeehouses in the area. In the subsequent feeding frenzy, bands like Veruca Salt that were unfortunate enough to get snapped up by the majors and land Top 40 hits in about five minutes were roundly dissed by pontificating purists for not paying their dues.

Rock clubs like Double Door, a sister act to the Chicago institution Metro, and the scenester haven the Empty Bottle entered the fray. Independent record labels like Touch & Go and Drag City spun out discs, and hometown producers like Phair's ex-bandmate Brad Wood and enfant terrible Steve Albini, who leads the noise machine Shellac, helped shape sounds coming out of Chicago. All kinds of unexpected and eclectic performers started buying one-way tickets to our town, from Welshman Jon Langford of the cult fave punk-cum–hard country Mekons (he started his own pickup band the Waco Brothers) to singer/song-writer Syd Straw of Golden Palominos fame to a regrouped Poi Dog Pondering, the Hawaii/Austin-originated world-music aggregation that's become perhaps the city's most popular live act. And beyond the local talent pool, just about every night of the week—now, as then—you'll find touring acts booked into small clubs and big arenas.

Chicagoans are such creatures of their beloved neighborhood bars that it's tough to roust them off their bar stools to get up on a dance floor. It helps if there's a simple, economy-size dance floor not too far from the beer taps. Big enough to shake out those legs but not so sprawling and elaborate that they feel that they've got to go shopping for Gucci knockoffs to look the part. When hip urbanites go out dancing, the last thing they want to do is head downtown on weekends to compete for parking with overdressed thrill seekers who called ahead for the proper expressway exit. They can stay cool in their own bars where deejays often spin an engaging mix: Mondays it might be lounge, Tuesdays old-school funk, Wednesdays classic country. You get the idea.

Getting Past the Velvet Rope

If you choose to dive into one of the big clubs where they still play Chicago's very own house music—and there are fewer of these places by the day—you don't have to worry about being hip enough or outrageous enough to get in. Midwesterners just don't have the patience for the elitist disco-era concept of plucking the clubbiest nightcrawlers out of the line. Chicago may have its roots as a cow town but the locals don't have much forbearance for cattle calls. If you can handle the cover charge, you'll get in. *Eventually*. On busy nights, be prepared to cool your platformed heels on the sidewalk outside a few of the biggest spots for an insufferably long time while patrons who are members or claim guest-list status sail right through the door. In these situations, it certainly might speed up things if, say, you show up leading a duo of black-clad friends wearing dog collars on a leash or some other outlandish get-up. If you're bold enough, you could blow past the line.

Dress codes are enforced not only to leaven the atmosphere and make for a special night out, but to keep out or reduce the possibility of gang conflicts at clubs attracting younger crowds. Fashion faux pas include gym shoes, ripped jeans, and baseball caps. Guys sans gals are persona non grata at big clubs.

Chicago Clubs

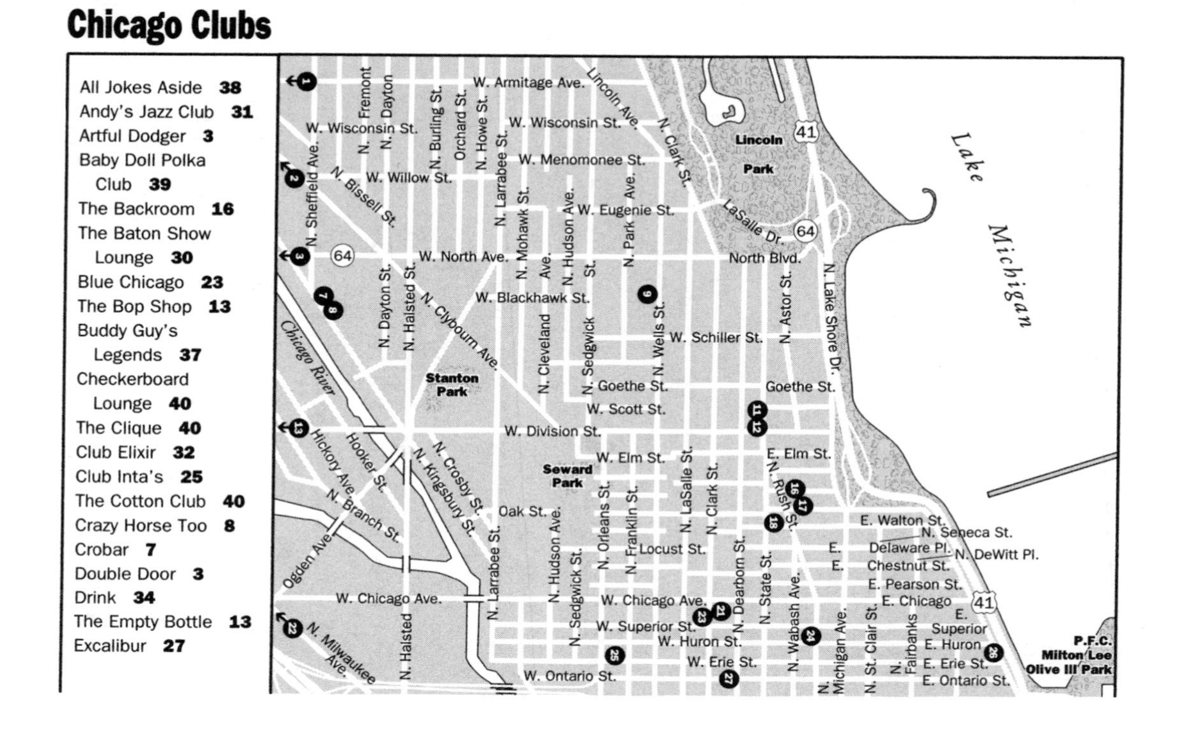

Exit **3**
The Generator **35**
Gentry of Chicago **24**
The Gold Star Sardine Bar **26**
Jazz Showcase **28**
Jilly's **17**
Joann's Piano Bar **21**
Red Dog **3**
Shelter **33**
Tania's Restaurant **22**
Tropicana d'Cache **1**
Underground Wonder Bar **18**
Whiskey River **2**
Yvette **12**
Yvette Wintergarden **36**
Zanies **9**
Zebra Lounge **11**

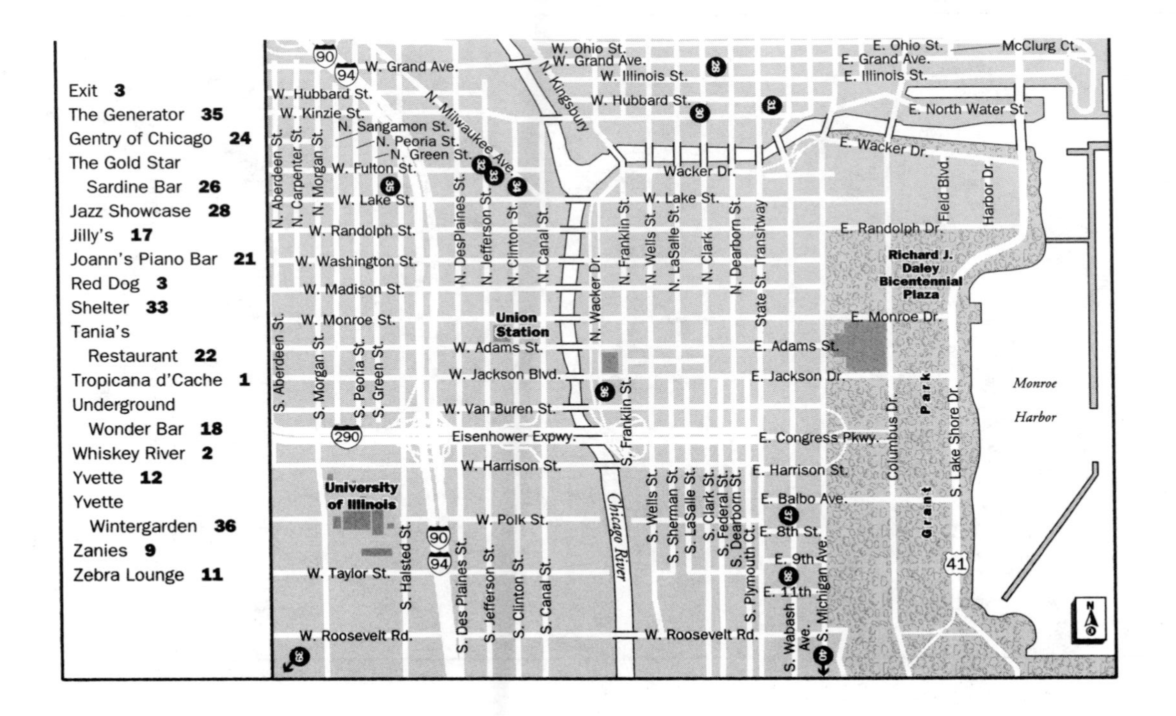

North Side Clubs

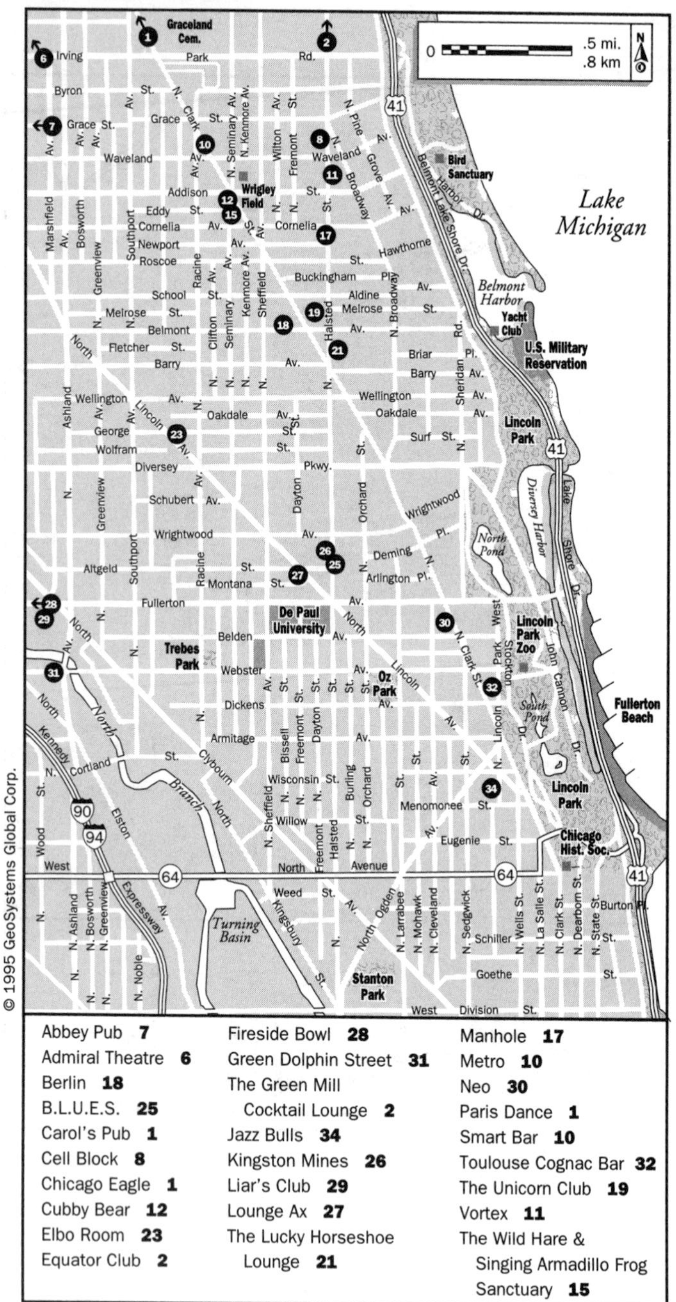

The Lowdown

All that jazz... It's pretty much impossible *not* to hear some jazz while you're in Chicago. There are scads of clubs devoted to it, and the high hats and horns seem to flow from just about every hotel bar in the city. After spending more than a decade at a faded downtown hotel, Joe Segal has taken his famed **Jazz Showcase**, the city's foremost jazz revue, to a classy new spot in River North—just in time for his fiftieth anniversary in the business in 1997. The split-level club has good sightlines for everyone, and the muted yellow walls show off black-and-white photographs of all the great ones who have played the club. The roll call is impressive, from Max Roach and Dexter Gordon to Wynton Marsalis. Nearby, the old standby **Andy's Jazz Club** dispenses with glamour in favor of a no frills, study-in-brown (carpet, paneling) room radiating with the glow of neon beer signs. A few Chicago Jazz Festival banners behind the stage brighten up things; but the journeyman decor of the wide-open room seems just right for the local players, tourists, and downtown workers who show up for the evening sets by mainstream Chicago acts kicking off at 5. You can sit at the horseshoe-shaped bar or closer to the stage at one of the white tablecloth-covered tables (and order a pizza or a prime rib dinner). The long gangway leading to **The Backroom** adds to the cozy, secluded feel of this appropriately named jazz club, a longtime fixture on Rush Street that's rebounded after a fire a few years back. Tuxedoed doormen escort guests—mostly out-of-towners and couples looking for a magical evening—to candle-lit tables at the stage's edge or one of the balcony seats where you get a bird's-eye view of the players (and their bald spots) below. But the most intimate jazz room in town has got to be the Gold Coast's **Underground Wonder Bar**, a tiny spot a few steps below street level that's fun and informal and gets a quirky late-night audience. On the South Side, **The Cotton Club**, a classy jazz room, has boosted the careers of a number of talents (including saxophonist Art Porter and R&B superstar R. Kelly). The white-walled room decorated with huge photos of jazz legends draws a predominantly upscale buppie crowd.

You don't have to know bop from cool to while away the night at **The Green Mill Cocktail Lounge**, a holdover from the days of jazz and bootleggers when Uptown was Chicago's swinging entertainment mecca. The onetime Capone hangout (he favored a spot with a view of the door; check out his photo on the baby grand behind the bar) has all of its Deco stylings intact from the thirties and once again is one of the liveliest jazz venues in town under Dave Jemilo's stewardship, with weekly big-band nights, after-hours jazz stylists, and top-notch combos. Nestle into one of the cozy velvet booths that add an air of elegance or find a perch at the long bar. At the self-consciously retro, forties-style **Green Dolphin Street**, an old autobody shop on the banks of the Chicago River has been transformed Cinderella-like into one of the city's newest and most sophisticated jazz clubs. The high-ceilinged ballroom has polished wood floors, a long black banquette along the maroon cinderblock wall, and everywhere else white tablecloth-covered tables arranged just so. Behind the dark wood bar model-y bartenders coolly take your drink orders. The big stage hosts all types: Latin jazz, acid jazz, 16-piece big bands, jam sessions. Bring your cigars and fedoras and be ready to pose. Critics complain the owners spent more money on decor than acoustics. A lone outpost in the alt.rock world of Wicker Park, **The Bop Shop** has an enterprising lineup that includes weekly "New Kids on the Bop" jam sessions and big band nights. Two arty chambers sit side-by-side: a cozy performance space with a bunch of tables, chairs, and an olive-colored banquette for kicking back and taking in the show; and a ruckus room with bar, pinball machines, and pool when you just want music in the background.

Homes of the blues... Chicago's famous for smoky blues joints where legendary musicians jam seven nights a week until dawn. A fixture for three decades, **Kingston Mines** in Lincoln Park keeps the music going without interruption on two cramped stages. The club has a smoky, ramshackle roadhouse feel—you can't help but wonder if the whole place is going to collapse at any minute—but it's exactly what you expect from a blues room. They like to brag about the latest celebs to drop in. Often it seems like more people stand in line here than go inside **B.L.U.E.S.** across the street, an intimate, one-room venue where a half-dozen tables sit just feet from the tiny stage. Serious blues aficionados and a handful of college kids watch Son Seals and others with worshipful attention. Lady blues belters like Gloria Hardiman and Big Time Sarah are the house specialty of **Blue Chicago**, a classy twenties-style club in the thick of River North where the brick walls are graced with evocative original paintings of Chicago blues vignettes (conveniently for sale on T-shirts). The club has even put out a compilation, *Women of Blue Chicago*, on Chicago's Delmark label. On the southern edge of downtown, **Buddy Guy's Legends** books both local talents and established stars (Dr. John, Junior Wells, and Buddy Guy himself). Packed with lively aficionados and partyers, the big open room is decorated Hard Rock–style with such blues memorabilia as a green-sequined dress worn by Koko Taylor in the fifties, a Muddy Waters tour jacket, portraits of Willie Dixon and Stevie Ray Vaughan, and tons of guitars owned by Eric Clapton and other 12-bar demigods. Guy usually plays a long, sold-out homestand here each winter. There's lots of room to find a place to watch the performers or shoot some pool. College students and locals share the shabby digs of the South Side's legendary **Checkerboard Lounge**, where pros like Magic Slim and the Teardrops take the stage seven nights a week. A secure parking lot is available across the street.

Disco emporiums... Once in a blue moon over Lake Michigan, a flashy new nightclub makes a buzz in Chicagoland. Likely, it's in a rehabbed warehouse on the edge of downtown. Yes, it *is* fun for the first few months. The rest of the story is predictable: Fickle scenesters grow bored and move on; and once the carloads of suburbanites show up, the fun is over. One of the first warehouse dance palaces put through the paces in the early nineties was River West's **Shelter**. Where other giants have fallen—China Club, Cairo, Ka-Boom!—this labyrinth club has an art director's touch that sets it apart. Bordello-red

Gothic fixtures cast a spooky pall over hallways connecting assorted dark chambers and hideaways illuminated by votives, lava lamps, and staticky TV screens. Part of the fun is exploring it all; eventually you'll find your way to the longer-than-it-is-wide dance floor where house music booms from speakers that double as dance platforms. Warning: The vintage neon hotel sign above the main bar that says TOURISTS WELCOME gives away more than it should. This club has long ago dropped off the social calendar of most urbanites, leaving the young trying-too-hard twentysomethings from the hinterlands dressed in body-hugging stretchy shiny clothes to face the ogrelike bandana-headed door bouncers. The other heavy hitter in Chicago is one of Dennis Rodman's haunts: **Crobar**, on the cusp of Lincoln Park, a club that's as open and cavernous as Shelter isn't. On weekends, look for the line of anxious trendoids snaking down Kingsbury along the railroad tracks—there's no sign out front, only huge neon Chinese characters. Walking in the door just screams this-must-be-how-it-is-in-New-York big-energy dance club. (Look, people dancing in a cage!) It's hard to tell where the dance floor begins and ends; and it's so big it should have its own missing persons desk.

You'll feel like you've stumbled into somebody's freewheeling after-hours party at **Red Dog**. The long and hard-to-see-through-the-haze sliver of a dance floor in Wicker Park is always packed for a mix of old school funk, house, and hip-hop. Up above there's a lounge perfect for rehydrating after a dance workout. Booths in the bar area peer down on the streetlife freak scene at the intersection of North, Milwaukee, and Damen. One of the newest warehouse hot spots west of downtown, **Club Elixir** is the kind of show-offish club where continental trust-fund kids park fancy Europeans cars out front. (Who needs to drive a Hummer in Chicago? *Puh-leaze.*) Around the corner at the cavernous, warehouse-cum–high concept funhouse **Drink**, it's one big frat rat mixer. Twentysomethings boogey to live bands, and deejays spin pop and alternative tuneage. A maze of open chambers includes a neo-primitive Tiki lounge with swings and a three-level smoking room complete with humidor, Dr. Suessian couches, and walls with tie-dye hangings. The upscale, dressed-to-impress black clubbers discoing at **The Clique** take the downtown club's dress code to heart (look smart, leave the ripped jeans and tennis shoes at home)—if they don't, the tuxedoed bouncers will let them know.

On the queer dance fever front, the runway-size dance floor at **The Generator** in River West has no problem filling up—though not until pretty late. Under the watch of the deejay's control booth, the largely gay and black dancers get lost in pounding house music. Need a break? A long, long bar flanks the left wall and a few pool tables are crowded. At the other big gay dance club in town, Lake View's **Vortex**, a cluster of disco balls straight out of *Saturday Night Fever* hang over the floor. The polysexual clubbers here mix and match races, sexes, incomes, everything; and the stage hosts touring disco divas like Marsha Wash and Jimmy Sommerville. You can watch it all from the catwalk above. Jaded? Try the karaoke bar. On a smaller scale, the gay disco **Berlin** has managed to retain its freewheeling spirit after more than a decade in business, luring thrillseeking straights and suburban lesbians alike on the weekends. The small Lake View dance floor gets crowded but always seems capable of absorbing more bodies. Just step into the throng. For a few glorious years of eighties high life, Chicago aped New York clubland with its very own Limelight. It's long since closed down, but Limelight's party grounds in the fortresslike former Chicago Historical Society building have reopened as **Excalibur**, complete with three dance spaces, including the adjacent "alternative" club, the Dome Room. A sprawling for-the-masses amusement center, Excalibur crawls with suburbanites and tourists who *do* look like they're having fun.

Bars with deejays... Don't be intimidated by the broken glass and spray-painted walls in **Neo**'s long alley entrance. It's faux urban blight. Inside this made-to-feel-gritty Lincoln Park club, concrete pillars and archways may remind you of a loading dock, but you'll be surrounded by De Paul students and clean-cut yuppies out for a nostalgic dose of eighties dance music. Thanks to the smoke machine mist, you won't be able to see them. With a playlist of The Cure and Nine Inch Nails, this is the kind of place where you dance by yourself. Remember your black eyeliner for the weekly goth and industrial nights. Chicago could use more bars like **Artful Dodger**, a Bucktown corner pub with vinyl booths up front near the bar for hanging out and a bare-bones black-lit dance floor in back for jamming to the deejay's mix of funk, soul, and hip-hop. The gay Uptown bar **Big Chicks** (see The Bar Scene) has emerged as a small alternative dance destination on weekends when you want to move to the beat of a familiar favorite—from an old Stones classic to early eighties fare tracked from a CD collection behind the bar.

Another standby is Wrigleyville's **Smart Bar**, a hideaway below the rock club **Metro** (see "Rock On, Wayne," below) that's remembered wistfully by aging New Wavers as a dark, raw, wide-open space where they swayed to the gloomy sounds of Bauhaus and The Smiths. In a heretical makeover, it's been yupdated for the nineties as a retro supper club with cheery orangish Venetian-style lamps and a dance floor ringed by booths. Music runs from acid jazz to funky club fare. At the Wicker Park club **Exit**, gloomy alternative and industrial music booms across a dance floor enclosed in chain-link fences. Tattoos and studded leather jackets are practically mandatory evening wear. Exit specializes in theme-park perversity: a half-dozen motorcycles parked in a row for drinkers to sit on, gas masks shining with red light, and other self-consciously morbid touches like nooses and paintings of Hitler, Sid Vicious, and John Gacy enjoying a cocktail. One of the latest neighborhood hot spots with an intimate dance floor is **Liar's Club**, a hipster bar on the cusp of Lincoln Park where lights flash beneath the clubber's thick-soled footgear. It has fez-like lamps, red Naugahyde walls, and a little velvet-curtained private nook off the dance floor. Don't miss the old Kiss pinball machine upstairs in the pool lounge.

Latin beats... **Tropicana D'Cache** delivers what you'd expect from a big Latin nightclub: high-energy orchestras on a stage backed with gold lamé and neon, expert dancers dressed to the nines, and plenty of cocktail tables over two levels for intimate conversation. An older, less flashy crowd moves to the beat in the shadows at the late-night Caribbean restaurant in Logan Square, **Tania's**, something of an institution in Chicago. During the day, Latino pols and businessmen have power lunches, and the hallway shows off pictures of the owner with local celebs and sports heros. The dance floor is oddly tucked away in an unlighted, low-ceilinged corner of the restaurant but that doesn't deter anyone from salsa-ing off their meal. In River North, **Club Inta's** is elegant and stylish all the way, from the sweet eucalyptus scent in the air to the leggy women in tiny black dresses and men in sharp silk shirts and trousers. This crowd executes seemingly choreographed moves to big band salsa and merengue twice a week. A halogen-lit warehouse space, it has free after-work buffets and, if you can't dance, salsa lessons.

If you like to jitterbug... If you're downtown to ascend the Sears Tower, make it an evening by stopping next door at **Yvette Wintergarden**, a plush jazz room where couples dance to combos each night. On warm nights, it turns into an open-air cabaret. A more informal scene is at **The Redhead Piano Bar** off Michigan Avenue, where you can sway to twinkling ivories and vocalists. There's no dance floor, but that doesn't stop people from standing up and expressing themselves on the carpeted floor.

Two-steppin' heaven... Chicagoans aren't the city slickers they'd always have you believe. Country music is big here. Many of the Nashville stars head to theaters and arenas in the burbs, but the high-concept **Whiskey River** club still brings in some big names like Jerry Jeff Walker and Confederate Railroad. Most nights weekend westerners work on their line-dance moves among all the wagon wheels, antlers, cow skulls, license plates, and millions of neon beer signs—it looks like someone raided the country-western section of the Bennigan's antique warehouse. At **Carol's Pub** uptown, you'd think the house band, South of Midnight, would feel unsafe without chicken wire sheltering the stage. When they're not too drunk (and even when they are), the hardscrabble regulars get up to dance. This is a real live honky-tonk, incongruously (and wonderfully) doing business right in the middle of Chicago.

Where the boys and girls go... The biggest gay disco on the Halsted strip, **Vortex**, has a big sweaty mess of bodies grooving to a big tribal beat. If you squint really hard into the hazy light, you'll find a young, multiracial army of adrenalin-charged barflies and a few shirtless muscle boys. Down the block, the leather-lite dance club **Manhole** is kinda sleazy, and that's precisely the idea. The lights are low, the decor is modeled after a sewer (really), and guys lurk about the dance floor bare-chested. (A large bar chamber in the back that takes up half the club has its own dress code of leather, uniforms, western wear, or T-shirtless torsos.) On the wildy popular monthly underwear nights, you can show off your Calvins and inspect everyone elses. Located at the foot of the Belmont el stop, **Berlin** hasn't shown any signs of tiring as one of Chicago's reigning danceterias. The young, preening crowd of guys and gals, drag queens, and other exhibitionists mingle and mix with abandon, a few stepping above the dance floor fray (it's so crowded that you can't even move your feet) to parade on platforms. Chicago's lesbians get chic at Uptown's stylish disco parlor **Paris Dance**, where everyone can watch the prominent but compact dance floor from the sidelines. Glamorous murals of twenties screen sirens and Sapphic femmes inspired by the painter Tamara De Lempicka grace the walls, and a smart deco cafe is the perfect place for a sit-down. Way downtown from the gay ghetto, **The Generator** lures a crowd of African-American men and a handful of women to its sprawling wooden dance floor in a River West warehouse.

Where boys will be girls... Wonder where Dennis Rodman learned how to work magic with mascara? Look no further than the showgirls strutting across the stage at **The Baton Show Lounge**, the city's celebrated female-impersonator revue. It's a tough call judging which is the more curious phenomenon—the made-up performers lip-synching everything from Pat Benatar to Whitney Houston, dressed in complicated sequined gowns (many of them designed to show off their hormone-induced breasts), or the fact that brides-to-be from the burbs throw their bachelorette parties here. It's totally surreal.

Piano bars... For campy dish and a lively happy-hour crowd, check out the piano artists at **Gentry of Chicago**, a gay bar located in a stately town house one block off Michigan Avenue. A huge chandelier dominates the front room, while a basement video bar draws a younger crowd. Amateurs step up to the open mike on Sundays. A change of pace from the mayhem of Division Street, **Zebra Lounge** is a dark, mirrored piano bar that takes its namesake as a decorating motif. It's small and the players are run-of-the-mill—but that's not why you're here. One of the newest players on the lounge circuit is **Jilly's**, the latest in a long line of clubs named for the late Jilly Rizzo, Frank Sinatra's pal and former manager. The stage is set way at the back of the dark bar, so patrons sitting at the window tables feel free to yak away, especially in warm weather when the windows open to the street. When the pianist or trio is taking a break, you can always amuse yourself by watching the model train wend its way around the top of the bar. At **Joann's Piano Bar**, the house's eightysomething pianist plays shouted requests, reading from tattered songbooks, while the funky, eclectic regulars and one-timers (who've all been drinking too much) sing along and occasionally grab the mike for solos. A bevy of chandeliers hang from the ceiling of this personality-plus saloon, which also has velvety wallpaper, old mirrors, vintage photos, and other musty paraphernalia.

Where the singers are... Everybody who's anybody and nobodies on their way to becoming somebodies have played the windowless, mirror-and-chrome **Gold Star Sardine Bar**, a fixture on the lounge circuit that's partly owned by New York piano stylist Bobby Short. They certainly got the name right here: This tiny Streeterville jazz cabaret will make you feel like, you know, a small canned fish. Top-flight vocalists from both Chicago and beyond perch on the baby grand to croon standards at **Toulouse Cognac Bar**, a super-intimate Lincoln Park club done up in—you guessed it—red velvet. A Toulouse-Lautrec reproduction hangs on the wall, and you can chomp peanuts in Empire chairs at tiny black cocktail tables. Off Division Street, **Yvette** is a handsome Deco-ish night cabaret for grown-ups. It's clear that everybody loves music at the **Underground Wonder Bar**, a funky little Gold Coast jazz club. You can hear a range of singing styles in one night here, from co-owner Lonie Walker's Janis Joplin–style rasping to your music-student waitress to maybe even Liza Minelli or another celeb drop-by. If the singing takes you to a magic, creative place, they supply crayons for placemat doodling.

Rock on, Wayne... Often destined for bigger arenas the next time they come to town, major-label rockers play the intimate **Metro** in Wrigleyville. It's the total rock-'n'-roll experience. Before they got too big for their britches, hometown heroes like Smashing Pumpkins, Liz Phair, and Veruca Salt played here. The grungy old theater is loud and raucous with a sometimes frenzied mosh pit, and everybody goes out into the night air after a show stinking of smoke with their ears ringing. Owner Joe Shanahan has expanded into Wicker Park with the **Double Door**, located at rock 'n' roll ground zero, the North, Damen, and Milwaukee intersection. The spacious club has some of the best acoustics in the city and a line-up of locals and hot new alternative acts like Soul Coughing Cornershop. Dark and velvet-draped, the high, pressed-tin ceilings and a beautiful long bar give it a dollop of class; there's plenty of standing room near the stage and a perch in the back claimed by early arrivals. It doesn't matter who's playing at the other major club in the vicinity, **The Empty Bottle**, because gabbing and drinking local hipsters fill it up every night of the week. Even if they are obscure, the national and hometown acts that play here have got impeccable indie credentials. A slightly higher-visibility roster of alternarockers, cult faves like Yo La Tengo and Girls Against Boys, play the cramped stage at the basement-like **Lounge Ax**, a Lincoln Park club that has benefited from excellent booking over the years by co-owners Sue Miller and Julia Adams. They may not stay put for long; the neighborhood has gotten squarer by the day and one cranky newcomer's ill-informed complaint has caused the owners endless hassles with the city. At benefit concerts and on one album, bands have raised money to help the club get out. A new location can only help things: Despite the high-caliber bands here, the long and narrow room makes it tough for vertically challenged music lovers to see the stage over the sea of heads. A lot of high school kids and a few Wicker Park scenesters check out shows on the small stage at the **Fireside Bowl**, a now-closed bowling alley, where underground punk bands register an 11 on the obscure-o-meter. The barn-sized **Cubby Bear** in Wrigleyville books a broad range of low-impact, safe AM rock and party bands—including the occasional big folkie or funk act—but on the weekends a lot of the twentysomethings just show up to revel. As its name indicates, this two-floor playpen absorbs post–Cubs games carousers and keeps them occupied with pub games. Darts, anyone?

Everything but the kitchen sink (live)... Schubas **Tavern** in Lake View puts its lovely antique meeting hall to good use: Folk and country singer-songwriter types of the Nanci Griffith/Lyle Lovett variety perform in this intimate setting for worshipful audiences. If you can get there early enough, the booths on each side of the room are the prime spots to watch a show. It can be kind of a drag to get stuck behind a big crowd in back of the room, but the front bar is a gregarious watering hole for neighborhood young 'uns. More pop-oriented country acts can be found at the C&W night club **Whiskey River**. An eclectic booking policy helps out emerging local talent at **The Bop Shop**, a boho music club in Wicker Park where there's always something cooking: big mambo orchestras, zydeco dance lessons, and, of course, the club's musical namesake. Lincoln Park's **Elbo Room** mixes and matches everything from acid jazz combos to pompadour-headed rockabilly throwbacks to a big band led by the octagenarian Barrett Deems, Louis Armstrong's former drummer. The bunkerlike music room downstairs has ambient lighting and intimate bench seats along the walls.

The global beat... Yo, leave your negativity at the door when you enter **The Wild Hare and Singing Armadillo Frog Sanctuary**, a reggae club inhabited by a mix of college kids in flannel and baseball caps, a few stylish African-American women with long braids, and square, overdressed suburban white couples who like to jam nevertheless, mon. Pretty much what you'd expect from a reggae club within the shadow of Wrigley Field. At the Uptown dance club **Equator Club**, a middle-aged crowd dressed in traditional African garb mix with those in jeans and T-shirts to the native sounds of calypso, soca, high life, and soukous. Tucked away in the basement of a Beaux Arts building, this bare-bones club has a few travel posters on the walls and about once a month books a live Afro-Carribean sensation. From the other end of the globe, Irish folk and rock acts like Black 47 and the Commitments, as well as stateside performers like Arlo Guthrie and Kris Kristofferson, are booked into the concert hall at the **Abbey Pub**, on the Northwest side, where there's a Sunday-night Irish jam. The Merry Makers, the house band at the Southwest Side **Baby Doll Polka Club**, are joined by the owner's son, Eddie Korosa, whenever he's not out touring. Until then, you can hear his records on the bar's juke. Middle-aged polka enthusiasts spin their big-haired gals around the tiny dance floor in this chaletlike room.

Where they take it all off... At least in public, your options in Chicago for gawking, gaping, or leering at nude or partially clad bodies of the same or opposite sex, whatever your pleasure, are pretty limited. **Crazy Horse Too** indulges its out-of-town, expense-account-enabled suits with all of the extravagances of a nineties "upscale gentleman's club": valet parking, tuxedoed doormen, pricey drinks, and three stages. The bevy of topless dancers circulate the chrome-and-mirrored room, wearing flesh-colored pasties. (The women have a lot of personality too: One gal spotted our notebook, peeled down her top, and chuckled, "Write this down!") Locals still can't stop calling the club by its former name: Thee Dollhouse. At the city's other major skin stage, the infamous **Admiral Theatre**, you won't be greeted by smarmy doormen, just a couple of kids working a ticket booth. The totally nude dancers here don't leave anything to the imagination, which is a good thing for the mix of business travelers, bachelor party celebrants, and your requisite troll types, who probably don't have much to spare. Somehow not surprisingly, straight women are out of luck in the city. They'll have to drive out to the suburbs to a male strip club, like the **Sugar Shack** (4003 West Blake St., Stone Park, 708/343–9660) out near the airport. **The Lucky Horseshoe Lounge**, a spiffed-up neighborhood gay bar in Lake View, showcases skinny G-string–clad dancers every night of the week. The mixed-age crowd gathered around the front bar here seems to appreciate the dancers amateurish bumping and grinding—or at least the camp value of it all. Older and more muscular beefcake types, the dancers at the nearby gay disco **Berlin** can't really dance to save themselves, but that doesn't seem to bother the gaggle of guys and girls surrounding the small center stage where they perform twice a week. Lesbians get their turn when female strippers take over at the club's twice-a-month "Women Obsession" nights.

If you like leather... The leather daddy of them all is the **Chicago Eagle**, a gay club in Andersonville that's a serious hangout for both seasoned veterans in chaps-and-mustache uniforms and curious clean-cut boys who picked up their leather jacket on sale at Banana Republic. The main bar upstairs is black and grungy with a pool table and a big-screen TV showing porn flicks. Pass the dress-code inspection—one article of black leather will do (and you can buy some at the in-club store if you don't)—and you're permitted to descend into "The Pit," a cave-like room with lots of shadowy corners. A younger leather crowd and voyeurs wanting to see what the scene is all about will find the new upstart **Cell Block** in Boys Town a brighter, less intimidating destination. Here the back room is called the "Holding Cell" and is the setting for "Fetish Fridays" when every predilection from ripped jeans to hoods and masks is indulged with demos and giveaways. Up front there are videos, dancing, and a leather shop. Leather is more of a fashion statement than a lifestyle at **Exit**, a Wicker Park club where pierced-and-tattooed grungesters in motorcycle jackets straddle choppers near the main bar. Occasional bondage nights see people getting tied up.

A walk on the wild side... There's nothing discreet about **The Unicorn Club** on Halsted Street, the city's foremost gay sex club for men. Regulars call it "the white-skirt palace," for the towels cinched around everyone's waists as they make the rounds. Members line up like moviegoers at the box office; once inside, they go to their assigned private room or roam through the two floors of TV, whirlpool, and steam room areas. There's a modest fee to join.

Laugh's on you... The stand-up comedy craze has (blessedly) cooled, leaving only a couple of clubs in the city standing. **Zanies** in Old Town reigns as the big professional comedy club in town, hosting marquee-name comedians from Showtime, HBO, Comedy Central, and the world of TV sitcoms. On the southern edge of downtown, **All Jokes Aside** showcases some very funny African-American and Latino comics, including stars from "Saturday Night Live" and "In Living Color" and folks from the where-are-they-now-file like Shirley Hemphill of "What's Happenin'?" They also do a weekly "Apollo Night," a take-off of the Harlem theater's famed variety revue, showcasing local jugglers, magicians, singers, and musicians.

The Index

The original 312 Chicago area code was scheduled to split up into 312 and 773 areas in October 1996; the following listings reflect the new codes.

Abbey Pub. Irish brogues abound at this neighborhood spot that books folk acts from Ireland and the states.... *Tel 773/ 478–4408. 3420 W. Grace St., Blue Line Addison el stop. Open until 1am weeknights, 2am Fri–Sat, midnight Sun. Live music $0–15 cover.*

Admiral Theatre. A movie palace that's been made over as a kind of sex mall: Besides the Deco-appointed theater, there are a video and sex paraphernalia shop in the lobby, booths for private viewing, and guest appearances by "adult film" stars. No alcohol served.... *Tel 773/478–8111. 3940 W. Lawrence Ave., Blue Line Jefferson Park el stop, then transfer to eastbound 81 Lawrence bus. Open until 3am Mon–Thurs, 4am Fri–Sat, 2am Sun. $22 cover including two (nonalcoholic) drink tickets.*

All Jokes Aside. A near South Side comedy club featuring a predominantly African-American roster of local acts and occasional out-of-town celebs five nights a week (including three shows on Saturdays). Phone reservations are accepted; or buy tickets in person through the box office after 6pm. Jeans and gym shoes are frowned upon.... *Tel 312/ 922–0577. 1000 S. Wabash Ave., Red Line Roosevelt el stop. $10–16 and two-drink minimum. Open Wed–Sun.*

Andy's Jazz Club. Two jazz bands play each night at this low-key downtown jazz spot.... *Tel 312/642–6805. 11 E. Hubbard St., Red Line Grand & State el stop. $3–10 cover.*

Artful Dodger. The booths at this dimly lit Bucktown bar are so comfy you may never get up to burn calories on the back dance floor. Deejays spin funk, jazz, oh-so-trendy lounge music—it all depends on the night.... *Tel 773/227–6859. 1734 W. Wabansia Ave., Blue Line Damen el stop. $2 cover Fri–Sat.*

Baby Doll Polka Club. Polka thrives here, and the house band, the Merry Makers, really gets things jumping on weekends.... *Tel 773/582–9706. 6102 S. Central Ave., Orange Line Midway el stop, then transfer to 63 W bus.*

The Backroom. A pretty cool sculptural piece of three-dozen or so horns welded together and signed by jazz greats who've played here adorns the stage of this romantic jazz club.... *Tel 312/751–2433. 1007 N. Rush St., Red Line Clark & Division el stop. Reservations recommended. $6–8 cover and two-drink minimum.*

The Baton Show Lounge. The best drag show in Chicagoland. Packed, with three shows a night on weekends.... *Tel 312/644–5269. 436 N. Clark St., Red Line Grand & State el stop. Wed–Sun. Reservations recommended. $8–10 cover and two-drink minimum.*

Berlin. A small room, really, but this gay danceteria maximizes its real estate with wall-to-wall stimuli: a mix of music and videos from New Wave to techno, mirrors to see how the reddish light is flattering you, mildly entertaining go-go boys and girls atop platforms, and freaks galore.... *Tel 773/348–4975. 954 W. Belmont Ave., Red Line Belmont el stop. Open until 4am. $3 cover weekends.*

Blue Chicago. You get two for the price of one at this fine blues club. The cover charge also admits you to its sister club, Blue Chicago on Clark (536 N. Clark St., closed Mon), two blocks south. Take a souvenir with you.... *Tel 312/642–6261. 736 N. Clark St., Red Line Chicago & State el stop. Closed Sun. $5–7 cover.*

B.L.U.E.S. Only 150 or so blues fans can shoehorn into this Lincoln Park blues joint, so get there before 9 or after midnight to get a seat.... *Tel 312/528–1012. 2519 N. Halsted St., Red Line Fullerton el stop. $5–$8 cover.*

The Bop Shop. You'll find some of the town's most adventurous booking at this cool Wicker Park jazz-and-everything-else music club.... *Tel 773/235–3232. 1807 W. Division St., Blue Line Division el stop. $3–8 cover.*

Buddy Guy's Legends. The Grammy-winning Chicago guitarist didn't just put his name on the sign out front: He owns, plays, and even hangs out at the bar of this acoustically superb blues hall, which also serves up Louisiana-style soul food until midnight.... *Tel 312/427–0333. 754 S. Wabash Ave., Red Line Jackson and State el stop. $5–16 cover.*

Carol's Pub. Westerns on the TV, a pool table, and a jukebox kicking out Dolly Parton, Alabama, and Alison Krauss. City folk with country in their heart will appreciate this divey, hillbilly tavern and its three-man house band.... *Tel 773/334–2402. 4659 N. Clark St., Red Line Wilson el stop or 22 Clark St. bus. Music starts at 9pm Thurs–Sun. Open until 4am.*

Cell Block. Only leather men are admitted to the back bar at this new Lake View lounge.... *Tel 773/665–8064. 3702 N. Halsted St., Red Line Addison el stop. Open until 2am Sun–Fri., 3am Sat.*

Checkerboard Lounge. Once the heart of a vibrant South Side blues scene, this comfortably decrepit 25-year-old room is a mecca for locals, tourists, and occasional rock stars. Music begins nightly at 9:30.... *Tel 773/624–3240. 423 E. 43rd St. $5–7 cover.*

Chicago Eagle. The city's original gay leather and Levi's bar attracts serious B&D enthusiasts. Don't worry if someone won't talk to you; they may be just a little tied up at the moment.... *Tel 773/728–0050. 5015 N. Clark St., Berwyn el stop on Red Line. Open until 4am.*

The Clique. A relaxed jazz lounge and comedy club downstairs, and a jammed discotheque upstairs.... *Tel 312/326–0274. 2347 S. Michigan Ave., Red Line Cermak el stop. Open until midnight weeknights, 4am weekends. $6–10 cover.*

Club Elixir. Don't mind the Eurotrash. This cooler-than-thou, stand-and-pose nightclub is all sexed up with velvet curtains and splashy paint finishes.... *Tel 312/258–0523.*

325 N. Jefferson St., Green Line Clinton & Lake el stop. Open Wed–Sat until 4am. $10–15 cover weekends.

Club Inta's. A heavily Latino and black crowd fills up the R&B and Latin dance nights here. Free after-work buffets and dance lessons for the salsa-impaired.... *Tel 312/664–6880. 308 W. Erie St., Brown Line Chicago el stop. $5–10 cover. Minimum age 25.*

The Cotton Club. Named for the Harlem club, this Downtown jazz spot puts on three or four sets a night. Believe it or not, the Monday open mike draws big crowds for often impressive vocalists. You can always escape to the dance club in back.... *Tel 312/341–9787. 1710 S. Michigan Ave., Red Line Cermak el stop. Open until 4am. $7–10 cover weekends.*

Crazy Horse Too. Tell your cabdriver to look for the schlocky Las Vegas facade of Roman nudie statues and columns at this strip club—oh, sorry, gentleman's club—conveniently located just minutes from all the downtown convention hotels.... *Tel 312/664–7400. 1531 N. Kingsbury, Red Line North & Clybourn el stop. Open until 4am. $10 cover after 7pm.*

Crobar. This bi-level dance factory has choice perches for spying on the roiling sea of boiling bodies on the dance floor—adventure-seeking yuppies and suburbanites disguised in their best alternative rags.... *Tel 312/413–7000. 1543 N. Kingsbury St., Red Line North & Clybourn el stop. Open Wed–Sun until 4am. $3–10 cover.*

Cubby Bear. One of Wrigleyville's bigger rock clubs. Save it for darts after a Cubs loss.... *Tel 773/327–1662. 1059 W. Addison St., Red Line Addison el stop. Closed Sun–Tues unless there's a Cubs game or concert. $5–10 cover.*

Double Door. A club with strong alt.rock booking. Galaga, Tron, and a trio of pool tables downstairs.... *Tel 773/489–3160. 1572 N. Milwaukee Ave., Blue Line Damen el stop. $5–10 cover. Open until 2am.*

Drink. It's got four wide-open large party rooms for standing around looking at your cohorts. Flavored vodkas and other beverages served in Mason jars make the club's name operative.... *Tel 312/441–0818. 541 W. Fulton St., Green Line*

Clinton & Lake el stop. Open until 4am. Closed Sun–Mon. $5 cover after 9pm Thur–Sat.

Elbo Room. Hang out on the couch upstairs for cocktails or descend downstairs to listen to a funky mix of live music.... *Tel 773/549–5549. 2871 N. Lincoln Ave., Brown Line Diversey el stop. $3–10 cover.*

The Empty Bottle. Bands take the stage late in the week—mostly rock but some decent jazz too. You're here to rant about how your temp job sucks. Even better, try the pasta at the attached late-night diner, Bite (See Late Night Dining).... *Tel 773/276–3600. 1035 N. Western Ave., Blue Line Western el stop, then transfer to 49 Western bus. $5–7 cover for bands.*

Equator Club. African dance music most nights; live acts about once a month.... *Tel 773/728–2411. 4715 N. Broadway, Red Line Lawrence el stop. Closed Mon–Tues. $5 cover, more for live music.*

Excalibur. Excalibur is a hit parade of the last decade's nightlife trends: down-home eatery, video arcade, pool hall, top-40 dance club, and comedy club. They charge more if you want to go to the upstairs dance floor.... *Tel 312/266–1944. 632 N. Dearborn St., Red Line Grand & State el stop. Open until 4am. $3–8 cover weekends.*

Exit. Once an underground punk haunt spot in Old Town, this club has taken its signature skull-and-crossbones logo to a more dangerous strip in Wicker Park (Is she a prostitute?). Lots of bourbons at the bar and a pool table.... *Tel 773/395–2700. 1315 W. North Ave., Blue Line Damen el stop. Open until 4am. $3-5 cover.*

Fireside Bowl. Save for a wheatpasted flier here and there, this ex–bowling alley on the Northwest Side doesn't do much advertising for its all-ages punk-rock shows. On occasion local heroes do low-key sets here. Call for a long list of upcoming shows... *Tel 773/486–2700. 2646 W. Fullerton Ave., Blue Line California el stop.*

The Generator. Nonstop infusions of house music keep the vast dance floor at this predominantly black gay dance barn busy.... *Tel 312/243–8889. 306 N. Halsted St.*

Green Line Clinton & Lake el stop. Open Wed–Sun until 4am. $2–5 cover.

Gentry of Chicago. A cruisy gay piano bar. Regulars flock to the cabaret, where music starts at 5:30pm. The newer Halsted Street outlet is smaller and less formal.... *Tel 312/664–1033, 712 N. Rush St., Red Line Chicago & State el stop; tel 312/348–1053, 3320 N. Halsted St., Red Line Belmont el stop. Open until 2am Sun–Fri., 3am Sat.*

The Gold Star Sardine Bar. Sure it's small, but the intimate setting gets you up close to the jazz and cabaret performers.... *Tel 312/664–4215. 680 N. Lake Shore Dr., Red Line Chicago & State el stop. Closed Sun. $5–7 cover plus 2-drink minimum, Thur–Sat.*

Green Dolphin Street. Cool jazz, cigars, cocktails... the whole retro deal comes together at this glamorous new nightclub.... *Tel 773/395–0066. 2200 N. Ashland Ave., Brown Line Armitage el stop. Closed Sun–Mon. $5–10 cover.*

The Green Mill Cocktail Lounge. This movie-set-perfect jazz club draws an eclectic crowd (all ages, classes, and races) to this gritty neighborhood. They have good taste: Charlie Chaplin and Gloria Swanson once hung out here. Sundays feature the long-running Poetry Slam. Get there early to get a booth up front.... *Tel 773/878–5552. 4802 N. Broadway, Red Line Lawrence el stop. Open until 4am. $3–7 cover.*

Jazz Bulls. Musicians are nose to nose with jazz lovers at this basement-level club in a neighborhoody block of Lincoln Park.... *Tel 773/337–3000. 1916 N. Lincoln Park West, 11 Lincoln bus. $5–10 cover. Open until 4am.*

Jazz Showcase. The oversize mug of Charlie Parker greets you in the lobby of the city's leading jazz club, where a tuxedoed staff tends to your drink orders. And check this out: It's a nonsmoking club.... *Tel 312/670–BIRD. 59 W. Grand Ave., Red Line Clark & Division el stop. Closed Mon. Open until midnight Sun–Thurs., 1am Fri–Sat. $15 cover.*

Jilly's. A great place to listen to the piano artist or just to soak up the atmosphere and study the framed pix of the Brat Pack, Don Rickles, Steve and Edie, and other loungeish luminaries.... *Tel 312/664–1001. 1007 N. Rush St., Red Line Clark & Division el stop. Open until 2am.*

Joann's Piano Bar. So far this charming, rowdy, friendly old spot has held off the tourist-friendly makeover transforming the rest of the River North neighborhood.... *Tel 312/337–1005. 751 N. Clark St., Red Line Chicago & State el stop. Closed Sun–Mon.*

Kingston Mines. With a pair of rooms, this nonstop blues club gets a band going on one stage while another is winding down. Shows begin nightly at 9:30pm.... *Tel 773/477–4646. 2548 N. Halsted St., Red Line Fullerton el stop. Open until 4am. $8–10 cover.*

Liar's Club. Wicker Park hip meet Lincoln Park clean at this new bar and dance club near both neighborhoods.... *Tel 773/665–1110. 1665 W. Fullerton Ave., Red Line Fullerton el stop, then transfer to 74 Fullerton bus. $2–3 cover some nights.*

Lounge Ax. Come early to this sliver of an alternative-rock club and plant yourself on the risers near the stage. Otherwise you're advised either to be (a) tall or (b) not at all concerned about seeing anything. You can console yourself knowing you'll have easier access to the bar and the photo booth.... *Tel 773/525–6620, 2438 N. Lincoln Ave., Red Line Fullerton el stop. $3–10 cover.*

The Lucky Horseshoe Lounge. It's not especially reassuring to know that patrons are required to check their coats for a buck, thanks to the threat of theft, at this stylishly decorated Lake View gay bar equipped with billiards, darts, and nonstop strippers.... *773/404–3169. 3169 N. Halsted St., Red Line Belmont el stop. 2-drink minimum.*

Manhole. Coats aren't the only thing the gay boys check upon entering this dance club: On the wildly popular monthly "underwear nights" patrons show off their Calvins and inspect everyone else's.... *Tel 773/975–9244. 3458 N. Halsted St., Red Line Addison el stop. Open until 4am. Drink minimum during the week, $3–5 cover weekends.*

Metro. A Chicago institution, this sturdy old theater can be crowded, sweaty, and smoky when you pack throngs of alternative-rock fans into the small space. Save on Ticketmaster fees by buying advance tickets at the club's box office. Shows sell out quickly; but Wednesday nights are cheap at $5, and give new bands a chance to stretch themselves on the big stage.... *Tel 312/549–4140. 3730 N. Clark St., Red Line Addison el stop. $6–20.*

Neo. A real survivor on the ever-changing clubscape, this dependable dance lair in Lincoln Park has settled down with a steady clientele of students and clean-cut locals and even the occasional Mohawk. They spin funk, industrial, and dance tracks.... *Tel 773/528–2622. 2350 N. Clark St., Red Line Fullerton el stop. Until 4am. $2–5 cover.*

Paris Dance. The modest-size dance floor at this elegant lesbian disco is ringed by a bar and a small cafe serving sandwiches and desserts.... *Tel 773/769–0602. 1122 W. Montrose Ave., Red Line Montrose el stop. $5 cover Fri–Sat.*

Red Dog. Down an alley and up a towering flight of stairs, the entrance to this funky Wicker Park dance pad sets the appropriate underground vibe. You'll be sweating up a storm before you know it. *Tel 773/278–1009. 1958 W. North Ave., Blue Line Damen el stop. Open until 4am. Closed Sun, Tue. $5–10 cover.*

Schubas Tavern. A smart blend of live folk, country and highbrow rock performers is the focus of this handsome old Schlitz saloon. Food til 10pm.... *Tel 773/525–2508. 3159 N. Southport Ave., Red Line Belmont el stop. $4–15 for live music. Open Sun–Fri. until 2am, 3am Sat.*

Shelter. It may be past its prime, but Shelter was one of the first giant warehouse dance clubs in Chicago. Three rooms, three deejays—and it still has good deejays. There's a dress code.... *Tel 312/648–5500. 564 W. Fulton St., Green Line Clinton & Lake el stop. Open Thurs–Sat until 4am. $5–10 cover.*

Smart Bar. After shows upstairs at the rock club Metro, this subterranean Wrigleyville dance parlor fills up. But otherwise the music—which runs from jungle to funk —is background noise for a sparse walk-in crowd playing pool or pinball. Free entry for those 21 and older with tix to rock shows upstairs.... *Tel*

773/549–4140. 3730 N. Clark St., Red Line Addison el stop. Open until 4am. Free many nights, $5 cover weekends.

Tania's Restaurant. A stylish Latino nightspot institution; an airy room with a fountain in the center and a dance floor tucked into one corner.... *Tel 773/235–7120. 2659 N. Milwaukee Ave., Blue Line Logan Square el stop. Open until 4am. $6 cover for men on weekends (for nondiners).*

Toulouse Cognac Bar. Tuxedoed waiters accent the elegance of this plush cabaret room. Two shows a night.... *Tel 773/665–9071. 2140 N. Lincoln Park West, Red Line Armitage el stop of 151 Sheridan bus. Closed Sun. $3–10 cover with 2-drink min.*

Tropicana d'Cache. Salsa and merengue pulse through this Latin nightclub. There's a strict dress code, but it's not hard to get the patrons—a mix of Colombians, Puerto Ricans, Mexicans, and a few token Anglos—to overdo it with gusto.... *Tel 773/489–0600. 2047 N. Milwaukee Ave., Blue Line Western el stop. Thurs–Sat. Open until 4am. $5–12 cover.*

Underground Wonder Bar. A funky little Gold Coast jazz club.... *Tel 312/266–7761. 10 E. Walton St., Red Line Chicago & State el stop. Open until 4am. $2–6 cover.*

The Unicorn Club. Like the unicorn, there aren't many gay bath houses around anymore; but this is one, complete with saunas, steam rooms, and private rooms. Condoms and safe-sex pamphlets are freely doled out.... *Tel 773/929–6081. 3246 N. Halsted St., Red Line Belmont el stop. $11–20 plus membership fee. Open 24 hours.*

Vortex. You can easily lose your friends at this two-tiered maze of bars and dance floors that has changing nightly themes. A gay disco.... *Tel 773/975–0660. 3631 N. Halsted St., Red Line Addison el stop. Open Fri–Sat. Open until 4am. $5–8 cover.*

Whiskey River. Enthusiastic Reba and Clint wannabes of all ages in 10-gallon hats and dude boots put on a spirited floor show. The deejays play C&W music, and the bar serves basic grub.... *Tel 773/528–3400. 1997 N. Clybourn Ave.,*

Red Line North & Clybourn el stop. Open Tue–Sat. $3–5 cover, more for concerts.

The Wild Hare & Singing Armadillo Frog Sanctuary. The city's biggest reggae club brings in performers—including big-name acts like Burning Spear and Shabba Ranks—seven nights a week to its large, raised stage.... *Tel 773/327–4273, 3530 N. Clark St., Red Line Addison el stop. Open until 2am. $5–7 cover; free Mon–Tues and before 9:30pm.*

Yvette. This upscale jazz room is a more grown-up alternative to the meat-market mayhem of Division Street.... *Tel 312/280–1700. 1206 N. State Pkwy., Red Line Clark & Division el stop. Open until midnight Mon–Fri., 1am Sat., 11pm Sun.*

Yvette Wintergarden. An older, well-dressed crowd shows up at this downtown French restaurant to dance to local forties-style jazz combos.... *Tel 312/408–1242. 311 S. Wacker Dr., Brown Line Quincy el stop. Open until 10pm Mon–Thurs, 11pm Fri, midnight Sat. Closed Sun.*

Zanies. Big-name talent and suburbanite birthday parties fill the room at this Old Town comedy club.... *Tel 312/337–4027. 1548 N. Wells St., Brown Line Sedgwick el stop. Reservations recommended. Closed Mon. Sundays are smoke-free. $12 plus 2-drink minimum.*

Zebra Lounge. The black-and-white color scheme translates into an unintentionally hip backdrop at this small, dim piano bar safely off Division Street. An irregular collection of characters gathers for nightly songfests.... *Tel 312/642–5140. 1220 N. State Pkwy., Red Line Clark & Division el stop.*

the bar

scene 2

They say Chicago's a city of neighborhoods, so naturally neighborhood bars are where Chicagoans go out drinking. There they know they'll find their favorite bar stool, the Bulls or Bears on the tube, the bartender who knows their name and beverage, and the same old familiar faces. Though you'll find some bar-hopping bon vivants looking for fresh and fashionable scenes, the place at the corner will do for most of us.

Bars aren't the only places where Chicagoans like to hang out, though; in recent years, the corner tavern has been joined by the neighborhood coffeehouse. Like a Seattle-on-the-lake, Chicago has been inundated with more than 200 cafes, espresso bars, and coffeehouses. There's even a monthly newspaper inspired by a love of coffee: *Strong Coffee,* which is full of poetry, prose, and reportage on the local caffeine scene.

The Beaten Path

Chicago's bar scene is organized a lot like Disneyland: You don't really need to have a special destination in mind, just a theme, a mood, a lifestyle. Then hit the strip that suits those parameters. Conventioneers, suburbanites, and ill-informed visitors patronize the nearly indistinguishable pick-up bars radiating from State and Division streets, the traditional hub of the **Rush Street area**, which still boasts some nice jazz clubs and piano bars, but has lately been evolving into a restaurant and retail area. Most of party culture has shifted south to the **River North** warehouse district, where a number of hot spots are located. Chicagoans avoid this area on weekends, thanks to the mobs of Wayne-and-Garthish burb dwellers, and prefer to stick closer to home. A few blocks of **Lincoln Avenue**, from Armitage to Fullerton avenues, have sprouted bars and live-music clubs pandering to clean-cut postcollegiate types. The crowd is basically the same farther north, along **Clark Street** in Wrigleyville—a few reggae clubs and slacker-ish contingents mix things up a bit, but the sports bar rules here. **Halsted Street** is one of the city's big party promenades, divided into both gay and straight turf. Gays claim the blocks north of Belmont Street, straights stick between Armitage and Diversey avenues. African-Americans congregate at a number of well-heeled nightclubs along Michigan and Wabash avenues in the **South Loop**. The spit-polished BMWs and motorcycles parked outside a couple of bars on **Damen Avenue** are a sign of things to come: Lincoln Parkers have found a beachhead in the bohemian mecca of Wicker Park, though they leave the neighborhood's rough-hewn artist types undisturbed at their respective dives. All this fragmentation doesn't mean Chicagoans don't cross boundaries, however. Choose carefully and you'll find a few places where there's a lot of mixing and mingling of people and cultures.

What To Order

Chicago is a city of beer drinkers, its drinking habits set a century ago by waves of hops-happy Irish, German, and Eastern European immigrants. Until Prohibition, beermakers like Schlitz and Pabst owned hundreds of their own neighborhood taverns in Chicago. A few of the architecturally impressive structures survive today, as bars like Schubas Tavern and Southport Lanes & Billiards (see Sports), though more often than not they've become dry cleaners, doctors' offices, Thai restaurants, etc. The proximity to Milwaukee certainly hasn't hurt beer's cause, either. When all is said and done, a brewsky simply goes better with brats and tailgates. You'll still find a lot of folks drinking Bud and Lite (once brewed here) and trendier Wisconsin suds like Stroh's-owned Leinenkugel (ask for "Leinie" if you want to seem like a local), but Chicagoans and Midwesterners, always a bit suspicious of new trends, are finally catching up with the coasts in their taste for microbrewed beers. Imports are well represented in Chicago at Ranalli's (see Late Night Dining), spanning the globe with 100 beers, and a selection of ales and ciders at British/Scottish pubs like The Red Lion and The Duke of Perth. The corner tavern, the kind of place with Old Style on tap, has been reinvented in hipper neighborhoods, with boutique-y bars like Hopleaf and Sheffield's Wine and Beer Garden where customers face a dizzying array of regional microbrews. (Consistent with the city's healthy skepticism toward anything fashion-forward, one local bartender has come up with a rating scale using beret symbols, one to four, to indicate the degree of pretension he observes in these pubs with all their precious beers.) The trend has been boosted by a couple of brewpubs in the city (Goose Island Brewing Company and Rock Bottom Brewery) and a pair of breweries manufacturing and distributing their own brews (Legacy from the Chicago Brewing Company and Golden Prairie).

All this is not to say that you can't have your pick of mixed drinks and wines at Chicago's many drinking establishments. Besides the usuals, a few specially exotic numbers should be noted: the gigantic martinis at Gibsons Bar and Steakhouse, cognacs at The Big Brasserie & Bar at the Hyatt Regency, bourbon at Delilah's, aren't-we-having-fun Cosmopolitans at swank Espial, and glowing Aqua Velvas at Artful Dodger (see The Club Scene).

Etiquette

Like most everywhere else in the country, the drinking age in Illinois is 21. Don't be *too* flattered if you're asked to show a picture ID—even if you're graying around the temples and laughably past drinking age, be prepared to prove it. The city has put the fear of God, well, more precisely, the threat of losing their liquor license in bar owners, and bouncers can be real sticklers in requesting driver's licenses.

If you're going to drive home later, remember that blood- and breath-alcohol levels of .10 or more are illegal in Illinois (the standard in about three-quarters of the states). Drivers who fail a Breathalyzer test automatically lose their driver's license for three months; six months if they refuse to take the test. Though a a first-offense conviction is rare, it could result in a year of taking the bus and mooching rides.

And remember, Chicago may be home of the blues, but it ain't New Orleans, where revelers tote their beverages in go-cups in the streets. Here, you've gotta drink up before you continue your pub crawl.

Bars stay open plenty late here. The bar universe in Chicago is divided into two constellations: those bars with 2am licenses, which allow the taps to flow until 3am on Saturday, and those late-night destinations with 4am licenses, that stay open until 5am Sunday morning, making welcome refuges after the others have closed. (Last call comes half an hour before closing time.) In the listings below, we note any place with a late-night license, as well as the odd few that close before 2am.

North Side Bars

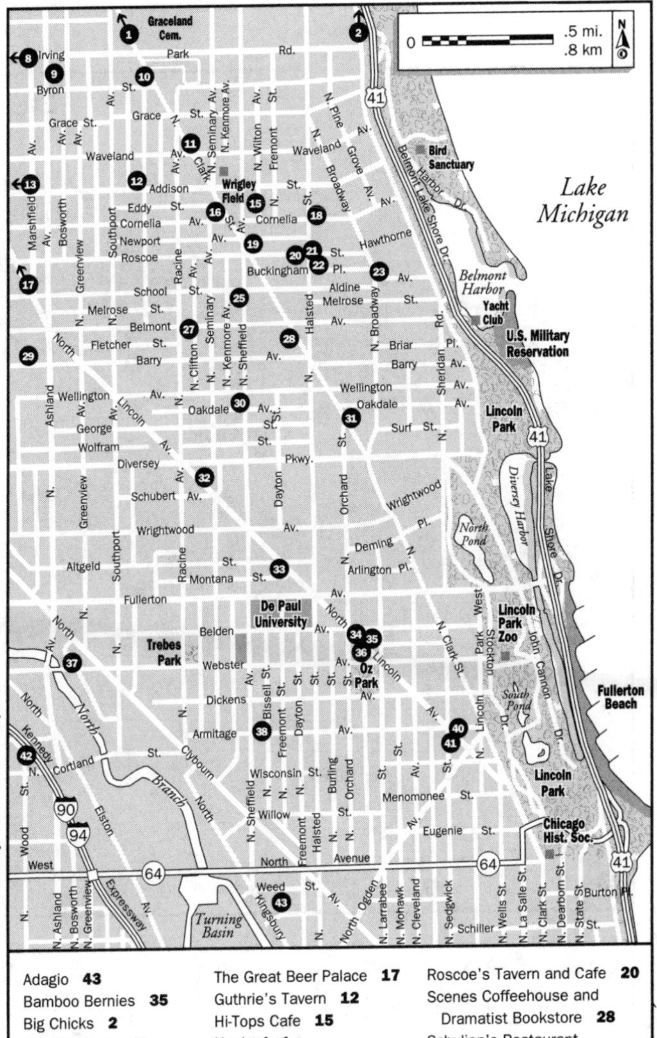

- Adagio **43**
- Bamboo Bernies **35**
- Big Chicks **2**
- The Big Nasty **36**
- The Closet **23**
- Cocktail **21**
- Cody's Public House **29**
- Delilah's **32**
- Don's Coffee Club **2**
- The Duke of Perth **31**
- El Jardin Cantina **19**
- Espial **38**
- Gamekeepers **40**
- Ginger Man Tavern **11**
- The Great Beer Palace **17**
- Guthrie's Tavern **12**
- Hi-Tops Cafe **15**
- Hopleaf **1**
- Interactive Bean **27**
- John Barleycorn Memorial Pub **34**
- Kopi, A Traveler's Cafe **1**
- Little Jim's **18**
- Marie's Riptide Lounge **42**
- No Exit Cafe and Gallery **2**
- Off the Line **1**
- The Other Side **13**
- The Red Lion Pub **33**
- Roscoe's Tavern and Cafe **20**
- Scenes Coffeehouse and Dramatist Bookstore **28**
- Schulien's Restaurant and Saloon **8**
- Sheffield's Beer and Wine Garden **25**
- Sidetrack **22**
- Sluggers **16**
- Stanley's Kitchen & Tap **41**
- Star Bar **30**
- Ten Cat Tavern **9**
- Uncommon Ground **10**
- Webster's Wine Bar **37**

Chicago Bars

The Berghoff **47**
Big Brasserie and Bar **42**
Billy Goat Tavern **39**
Bluebird Lounge **3**
Blue Note **1**
Buckingham's **50**
Cactus Bar & Grill **48**
Cité **40**
Coq d'Or **26**
Danny's Tavern **6**
Excalibur **34**
Frontera Grill **38**
Get Me High Lounge **6**
Gibsons Bar and Steakhouse **23**
Goose Island Brewing Company **2**
Green Orchid Room **45**
Hana Lounge **41**
House of Beer **18**
Howard's Bar and Grill **35**
The Hunt Club **22**

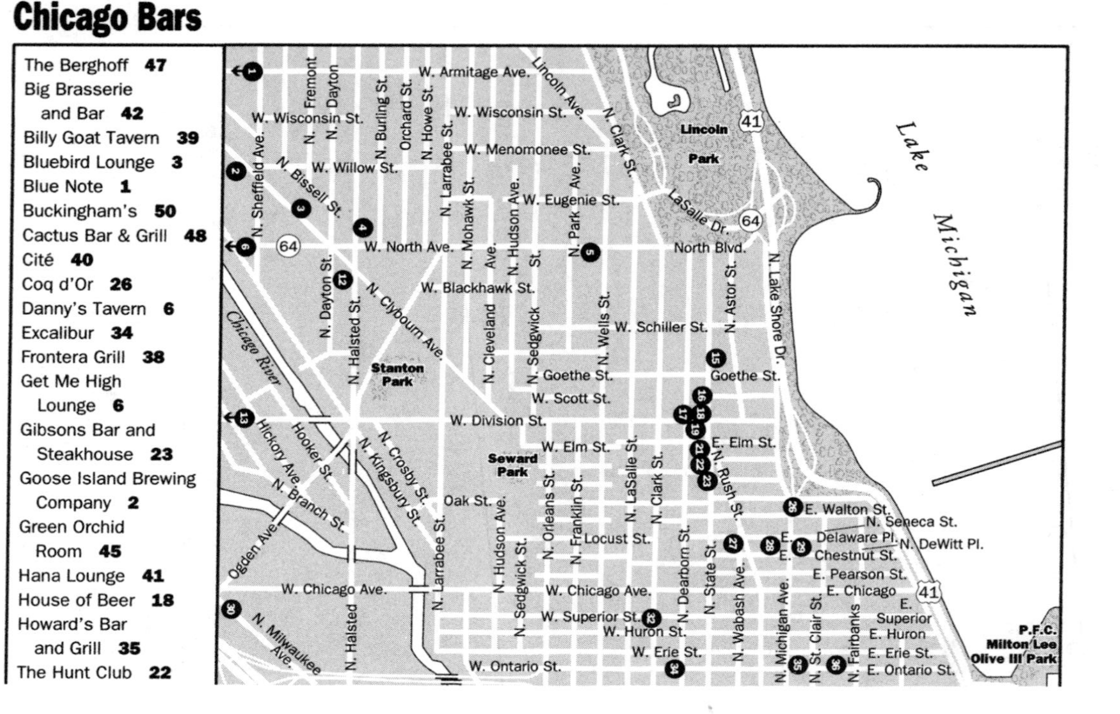

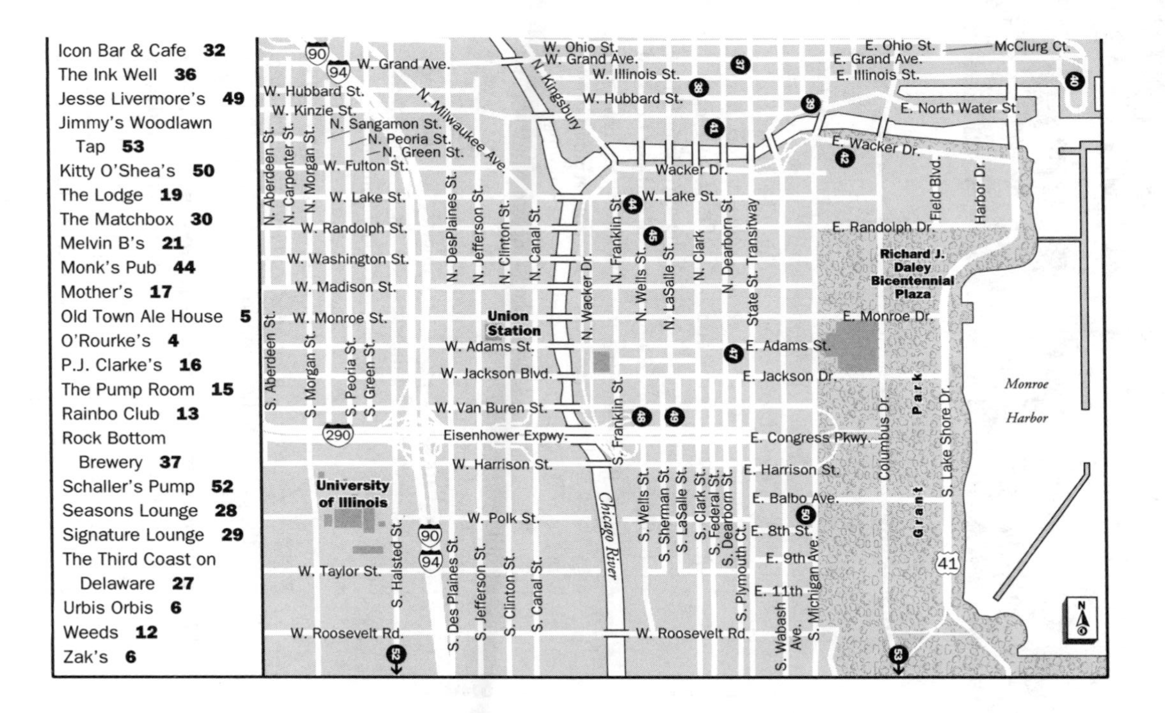

Icon Bar & Cafe 32
The Ink Well 36
Jesse Livermore's 49
Jimmy's Woodlawn Tap 53
Kitty O'Shea's 50
The Lodge 19
The Matchbox 30
Melvin B's 21
Monk's Pub 44
Mother's 17
Old Town Ale House 5
O'Rourke's 4
P.J. Clarke's 16
The Pump Room 15
Rainbo Club 13
Rock Bottom Brewery 37
Schaller's Pump 52
Seasons Lounge 28
Signature Lounge 29
The Third Coast on Delaware 27
Urbis Orbis 6
Weeds 12
Zak's 6
W. Ohio St.
W. Grand Ave.
W. Illinois St.
W. Hubbard St.
W. Kinzie St.
N. Sangamon St.
N. Peoria St.
N. Green St.
W. Fulton St.
W. Lake St.
W. Randolph St.
W. Washington St.
W. Madison St.
W. Monroe St.
W. Adams St.
W. Jackson Blvd.
W. Van Buren St.
Eisenhower Expwy.
W. Harrison St.
W. Polk St.
W. Taylor St.
W. Roosevelt Rd.
N. Aberdeen St.
N. Carpenter St.
N. Morgan St.
N. Milwaukee Ave.
N. Kingsbury
N. DesPlaines St.
N. Jefferson St.
N. Clinton St.
N. Canal St.
N. Wacker Dr.
N. Franklin St.
N. Wells St.
N. LaSalle St.
N. Clark
N. Dearborn St.
State St. Transitway
Wacker Dr.
Union Station
University of Illinois
S. Aberdeen St.
S. Morgan St.
S. Peoria St.
S. Green St.
S. Halsted St.
S. Des Plaines St.
S. Jefferson St.
S. Clinton St.
S. Canal St.
Chicago River
S. Franklin St.
S. Wells St.
S. Sherman St.
S. LaSalle St.
S. Clark St.
S. Federal St.
S. Dearborn St.
S. Plymouth Ct.
S. Wabash Ave.
S. Michigan Ave.
E. Ohio St.
McClurg Ct.
E. Grand Ave.
E. Illinois St.
E. North Water St.
E. Wacker Dr.
E. Randolph Dr.
Field Blvd.
Harbor Dr.
Richard J. Daley Bicentennial Plaza
E. Monroe Dr.
E. Adams St.
E. Jackson Dr.
E. Congress Pkwy.
E. Harrison St.
E. Balbo Ave.
E. 8th St.
E. 9th
E. 11th
Columbus Dr.
Grant Park
S. Lake Shore Dr.
Monroe Harbor
90
94
290
41
N

The Lowdown

Jam-packed... A hand on a shoulder here, a hand on a waist there—depending on your mood or blood-alcohol level, some Chicago bars can be a living hell or a total blast (especially on weekends, when tourists descend). Claustrophobes should steer clear of **The Matchbox**, a sliver of a Ukrainian Village bar where it doesn't take long to reach the fire code limit. The owner calls it Chicago's "most intimate bar," and he ain't lying: There are barely 20 stools lined up at the bar, and not much of an aisle to pass behind them. But the space has been maximized with a connoisseur's selection of microbrews, wine, tequilas, and cigars; candles behind the bar, street lights streaming through the large picture windows, and friendly expert bartenders add to the ambience. On popular Thursday nights, the young dressed-up crowd at Lincoln Park's **Adagio** is relentlessly in your face. Upstairs, disco music competes with the din of conversation, and people move you around like furniture to get to where they want to go. A critical mass of college kids do what college kids do at the juvenile Lincoln Park bar **The Big Nasty**: throwing back beers and spraying each other with the cans of Silly String sold here.

When you want a private conversation... The **Hana Lounge** in the Japanese-owned Hotel Nikko, on the north bank of the Chicago river, is quiet and serene enough to bring you to a Zen-like bliss. The sunken black couches are so cushy you won't want to get up, and the outdoor Japanese garden will make you forget you're in the middle of the city. Great exotic munchies, too (by Midwestern standards), like eggplant and skewers of beef, chicken, and shrimp. Couples seek out the snug booths of the **Bluebird Lounge** in West Lincoln Park, their faces lit by pools of light from funky fifties lamps. It's easy to miss the small blue neon sign in the Bluebird's window; inside, it's one of the darkest bars in Chicago, with a rustic Wisconsin north-woods look—flea-market paintings of fishermen and deer, forest-green walls, and a black tin ceiling. Impossibly darker still is nearby **Weeds**, which looks from the outside as if it had had a power outage; once inside, you'll find you're in one of the trippiest bars in the city. Psychedelic posters cover the walls, bras hang overhead, Mexican blankets drape from the bar, and beer taps are ornamented with big rubber figures of Donald Duck and Ronald Reagan. The right romantic lighting sets the mood at the **Star Bar** in Lake View, one of the prettiest bars in the city. Up front a constellation of starlike fixtures hang overhead; in back there's a fireplace surrounded by sleek built-in couches. Come here if the occasion calls for a glass of bubbly—the wine list offers lots of champagnes. It's easy to make yourself at home at **Danny's Tavern**, a popular Bucktown bar spread over an old Victorian two-flat (that's two stories, for you out-of-towners). From the small, first-floor rooms to the kitchen and outdoor deck upstairs, there are private parties happening all over the house—take your pick.

Dressing up... A jacket is required for entree into Chicago's legendary **Pump Room**, a glittering Gold Coast restaurant famed for its big booths and photo gallery of celebs (from Judy Garland to John Wayne) who have sat in Booth One. A solid dark-paneled bar tended by the tuxedoed staff overlooks it all. Taking the dress code to heart, the older coupled-up crowd and a handful of prowling singles go cheek-to-cheek on the dance floor. From fussing over your shiny European car with the valet to greeting the host, it's all about entrances at **Gibsons Bar and Steakhouse** on Rush Street. This high-roller scene is more casual, yet still the kind of place where you have to dress to get noticed: Men in expensive suits wearing lots of rings drink martinis with women in slinky bare-shouldered dresses. Later, everybody goes home to air out their clothes from the cigar smoke. The mood is less frenzied at the clubby piano bar **Coq d'Or**, but its location in the venerable Drake Hotel gives it a kind of nostalgic ambience recalling a time long before casual Fridays. Partygoers in tuxes show up here after their soirée in the ballroom. In Lincoln Park, a very put-together young crowd of marketing execs at **Adagio** dress to impress, giving the stylish Italian-restaurant-turned-nightspot the look of an oil slick, with all those leather jackets. The crowd is coiffed enough to make you want to run out and buy stock in a hair-gel company.

Dressing down... In this city, dive bars are as common as crooked politicians, and most aren't particularly memorable places. But a few, by virtue of an especially ruinous decor or eclectic clientele, make interesting destinations. Just a block off the Mag Mile, **The Ink Well** is a welcome sight amid the locale's high-gloss shine. Once a hangout for graphic design and advertising types (hence the name), the garden-level bar hasn't changed much since it opened more than three decades ago. The same old airport-lounge furnishings and gold laminated tables with, yes, ink spots, have transcended tackiness. A wooden streetscape behind the curved bar depicts the block when the bar first opened, more than 35 years ago. Windowless and downtown under the el tracks, **Monk's Pub** is the kind of place you'd never know existed. But inside, a funky melting pot of people inhabit the dark, narrow bar with a high black pressed-tin ceiling, pool table, blaring jukebox, and ancient wooden booths hugging the wall. The intimate **Get Me High Lounge**, smack up against the el in Wicker Park, is worth mentioning, and not just for its oddball name: The walls and ceiling are covered with chalkboards where patrons free associate, and you have to climb over an unused stage to reach the bathrooms. Another haunt in the same neighborhood is **Zak's**, a decrepit den where the bartender looks like Abraham Lincoln and artsy twentysomethings mix it up with the old-timers. The back room is a dormlike rumpus room of couches and chairs around a pool table.

Meeting the opposite sex... The pleasant, retro Southern roadhouse **Stanley's Kitchen & Tap**, in Lincoln Park, has as many fraternity and sorority alums underfoot as cracked peanut shells littering the floor. Packs of tall guys and lots of Tori Spelling blonds scan the scene at **Adagio**, a trendy Lincoln Park restaurant where a sort of Milanese modern creates the setting for a furious night of mingling, beautiful young professionals.

Everybody looks vaguely like someone from the cast of "Friends," except a few customers who look like Michael Jordan and Dennis Rodman, because they *are* Michael Jordan and Dennis Rodman. When folks start losing more of their hair, they start showing up at **Gibsons Bar and Steakhouse**, a high-profile Gold Coast spot where a more mature crowd puts the moves on each other. This decidedly nineties spot pays homage to the forties, with a handsome bar and bartenders in starched white shirts and solid black ties. Wraparound windows lend a view of the busy street life. On weekends, Lincoln Park yuppies take their BMWs and their mating dances to Wicker Park's popular late-night eatery and bar **The Northside Cafe** (see Late Night Dining). The terrific beer selection at **Sheffield's Beer and Wine Garden**, in Lake View, means you've got to do better than Bud when ordering a brew for that special someone you've just met. The scene reaches its peak in the summer out in the beer garden. The fabled Rush Street singles scene is enshrined at **Mother's**, a basement-level bar where guys who look like they dressed for the mall sit on bar stools with looks of expectation in their eyes. They just rented *About Last Night...* and think they're going to meet Demi Moore tonight. (After all, in the movie she met Rob Lowe here.) For a more nineties take on the same scene, **The Hunt Club** offers lots of perches for seeing and being seen. The bouncers make guys tuck in their shirts before entering this Rush Street nightspot. Good thing, too—did those slobs really think those babes in midriff-baring tops were going to pay them any attention? **P.J. Clarke's** is a big, airy saloon opening onto the street, giving you a view of the singles scene inside, slightly more mature than the meat market at its Division Street neighbors. Don't be fooled by how historic it looks—it's a Disneyland-esque creation by restaurateur Rich Melman and his Lettuce Entertain You group—but the massive oak bar and super-high ceiling spinning with fans still create a pleasant old-time ambience.

Meeting the same sex... A quiet Uptown neighborhood bar during the week (even drawing seniors from the high-rise across the street), friendly **Big Chicks** draws a packed house on weekends, when you'll often find the gracious owner greeting customers by name at the door.

It's a sea of gay men and fewer women going with the flow; you can't help but make the acquaintance of someone standing next to you. On Halsted, **Roscoe's Tavern and Cafe** is a local standby. Every gay man within walking distance shows up here at one time or another, so you're bound to run into that mysterious stranger you've been watching from afar. Once introductions have been made, you can disappear onto the dance floor in back. Nearby, some of the most attractive gay men in the city are installed, muscled bicep to muscled bicep, at the slick video bar **Sidetrack**.

No attitude or outfit is necessary to mix with the locals at **The Closet**, a mostly lesbian Lake View hangout. The best seats in this basic black box are the bar stools with a front-row view onto Broadway. Dig the bartender's famously bleached and spiky coif. The downtown newcomer **Icon Bar & Cafe** welcomes lesbian customers smack in the middle of the straight River North entertainment zone. Its hotel-bar aesthetic includes a prominent awning.

Spots to drink, downtown... The Loop isn't an area of the city that readily comes to mind when most Chicagoans draw up lists of places to go out. But if you can't stray too far from your lodging, downtown does have a few options that improve upon the usual soulless hotel bar or forgettable corner tavern. The bar at **The Berghoff** is Chicago's number-one bar—that is, the first saloon in the city to get a liquor license after the repeal of Prohibition. For its historical flavor and central location, the dark, oak-paneled bar remains a lively after-work destination for a suit-and-tie crowd. The Bismarck Hotel went for nostalgia with its cute little bar, the **Green Orchid Room**. The bartender does magic tricks and the cocktail waitresses (the "Green Orchid Girls"), clad in pouffy short satin skirts—very Emerald City—double as lounge singers. It's a bit gimmicky, but a fun place to have a drink to start the night. **Kitty O'Shea's**, at the Chicago Hilton and Towers, manifests its Irish theme with bartenders who actually hail from Dublin and know how to pour a Guinness, as well as traditional Irish acts that get the place doing such a jig, you forget that you're in a hotel bar. (We actually heard some Irish blokes crowing about a recent soccer match, "We beat Scotland!") **Big**

Brasserie and Bar, in the airy atrium lobby of the Hyatt Regency, gets its name because, well, it's really, really big. No problem elbowing up to the bar here—it's 228 feet long. Bartenders scamper up 15-foot-tall brass ladders to fetch top-shelf liquors for young consultants and middle-aged men with name tags on their loud blazers. Scaled way down is **Jesse Livermore's**, an English study of a bar with friendly service, where an after-work crowd unwinds in the financial district. Happy hour starts mid-afternoon, as soon as trading closes. One of the more colorful spots in the Loop is **Monk's Pub**, a hole-in-the-wall plastered with faded publicity stills of Marilyn Monroe and other movie starlets. Here, young traders sidle up to the bar alongside construction workers. It's a lunchtime favorite for its house chili and burgers, but some people do stick around after the Loop's cleared out.

Local color on the South Side... A Hyde Park institution, **Jimmy's Woodlawn Tap** is a grungy grad student bar that hosts occasional improv performances and prose readings. Operated by the same family for generations, **Schaller's Pump** is the quintessential Bridgeport bar, where locals from the Daley family's original stomping grounds gather for dinner served on vinyl red-checked tablecloths and sit around watching the Sox or the ten o'clock news. Check out the peephole on a side door, a sign of this century-old bar's Prohibition past.

Where gangsters hung out... Some of the city's oldest bars rode out Prohibition and proudly wear the vestiges of their speakeasy past like a badge of honor. Of course, you can't talk about Chicago and drinking without mentioning homeboy Al Capone; a few bars and clubs even display photos and mementos of him. Scarface's visage greets you at the door at **Schulien's**, an old German restaurant and bar in Lakeview that ran a speakeasy supplied by Capone during the dry years. Chicago history is laid on thick here, from the firefighters' helmets hanging from the walls to the photo gallery of Chicago celebs and sports stars. Meanwhile, the vintage English-style **John Barleycorn Memorial Pub** occupies a century-old Lincoln Park building that has functioned as a bar for much of its life, from twenties speakeasy to favored watering hole of John Dillinger.

Bars with an accent... Chicago has plenty of bars with Irish names and fewer with actual Irish customers. Locals join the conventioneer crowd and get rowdy at **Kitty O'Shea's**, the Chicago Hilton's large Irish-themed bar dressed up with photos of Irish castles and shillelaghs from Chicago St. Pat's parades. Whether or not you're going to dine on fish and chips, **The Duke of Perth** is a fine neighborhood destination in Lake View for conversation and drinking one of the ales or hard ciders from Scotland and England on tap. The pub, owned by two Scottish cousins, has one of the best selections of single-malt scotch in the city. Bedecked with Union jacks, photos of Churchill, paper pounds taped above the bar, and other Britophile bric-a-brac, the **The Red Lion** in Lincoln Park attracts locals of all ages for conversation over British beer and cider. Supposedly haunted, it's featured on a tour of supernatural Chicago, and the British owner—a former architect and WWII POW—is ready with stories of mysterious footsteps, voices, apparitions, and feelings of possession. Most of these phenomena have happened in the second-floor Churchill Room, so stick downstairs if you're afraid of being spooked. One of the oldest bars in the city, the German restaurant and pub **Schulien's Restaurant and Saloon** has a beautiful long oak bar backed with stained glass and beer steins and its own beers on tap.

Under the stars... Besides the city's raft of beer gardens (see "Beer here," below), a handful of drinking establishments offer open-air seating in fair weather. Located a block off Michigan Avenue, a woodsy rathskeller called **Howard's Bar and Grill** conceals a tiny brick patio in back where it's easy to forget you're in the heart of the city. The deck at the gay video bar **Sidetrack** provides a pretty nice way to enjoy the nighttime air, and the only place to get away from the ubiquitous TV screens inside. Beautiful people make the scene on Rush Street, at the sprawling sidewalk cafe in front of **Melvin B's**, where you'll find them working their designer shades even after dark.

Rooms with a view... The **Signature Lounge** has a vista that beats any other bar stool in the city: the ninety-sixth floor of the John Hancock Center. You won't even notice the sky-high drink prices. The view, especially facing south, is stunning—but not always (it's worth a call to check on visibility). The next best thing is the sight from the little cocktail area in Lake Point Tower's seventieth-floor restaurant, **Cité**. The place looks like something out of "Dynasty," and on a quieter night you may find divorcées chewing on each other's tonsils, but just keep your eyes focused on the vertigo-inducing view down onto Navy Pier, the Hancock Center and the lights north along Lake Shore Drive, and the dark expanse of the lake.

Playing around... Cabin fever can really get you down in a city where summer zips by in what seems like six weeks, but a few clever bars do their best to console with an array of indoor entertainment. The psychological implications of drunk postcollegiate guys vigorously spraying their button-nosed female companions with cans of Silly String are worth considering at **The Big Nasty**, a frighteningly popular Lincoln Park bar that can't keep the stuff on the shelves at $3.75. Darts are played with a passion at **The Other Side**, a North Side working-class lesbian hole-in-the-wall identified only by a few neon beer signs. Individual TVs are oddly placed at tables so patrons can watch what they want. Through the windows of an old house in Lake View, silhouettes of customers at **Guthrie's Tavern** lean earnestly over tables, warmed by the glow of small table lamps. Once inside, you'll see what they're up to: Every table is filled with postcollegiate types regressing to their not-so-distant childhoods, thanks to the bar's stockpiled shelves of board games from Battleship to Chutes and Ladders. **No Exit Cafe and Gallery**, the ancient coffeehouse in Rogers Park, is a mecca for Go players, and rents assorted other games like chess and Scrabble for 50 cents an hour.

Sports and suds... For starters, take your pick of most any place within a foul ball of Wrigley Field, most notably the **Cubby Bear** (see The Club Scene), a stadium-size bar and rock club that fills up with fans before and after Cubs games, or slick, pennant-festooned **Hi-Tops Cafe**, a bar topped with satellite dishes. Hi-Tops' crowd overflows onto the sidewalk during Saturday-afternoon gridiron games. You can also practice a few swings of your own, upstairs in one of the batting cages at **Sluggers**, a Wrigleyville megabar loaded with sports memorabilia. Sluggers seems geared for fans with a serious case of attention-deficit disorder: Downstairs there's a large bar, a grill with a good burger selection, zillions of TVs, a dance floor, pool tables, video games, Foosball, and bad rock bands performing; the upstairs midway-size arcade area (where you don't have to be 21 and alcohol isn't permitted) is outfitted with stuff like Skeeball, basketball and football tosses, video games, pinball, blah, blah, blah. The prototypical sports scene is **Gamekeepers**, a wood-paneled Lincoln Park bar with every game going on its multitudinous screens. For a more downtown crowd, try **The Hunt Club**, a Rush Street saloon with wide-screen TVs and a spacious bar in its airy main room.

A good neighborhood hangout is **Off the Line**, a no-frills sports bar in Ravenswood where local lesbians, gay men, and straights happily coexist most of the week. It gets as rowdy as any other sports bar when the Bulls or another Chicago team are playing. On Fridays and Saturdays, the clientele changes, as sweaty flag-football and softball teams show up to commiserate/celebrate after their games.

For stockbrokers... After a day of wild gesticulations on the floor of the city's commodity exchanges, cocky traders wrap their hands around a beer at the nearby **Cactus Bar & Grill**. The hybrid Tex-Mex cantina-sports bar, which hawks T-shirts with slogans like "Don't Drink and Trade," helps everybody unwind with colorful Christmas lights and music so loud that to be heard you have to shout directly into your drinking partner's ear. Using old wooden electrical spools for tables, it serves up pretty good frozen margaritas, a free happy-hour taco buffet, pool tables, and lots o' TVs. Upper-level execs do their moving and shaking in the more sedate environs of **Jesse Livermore's**, a paneled bar across the street from the Chicago Board of Trade. Decorated with brass chandeliers, dark velvet curtains, and equestrian prints, this classy and intimate lounge is a nice downtown retreat, whether or not you lead the wheeler-dealer life.

For writers and actors... The proximity of the Steppenwolf and the Royal George theaters has made

O'Rourke's, in Lincoln Park, a hangout for actors and writers. Presided over by huge yellowing photographs of Irish literary giants like Yeats, Wilde, and Joyce, O'Rourke's still feels like a neighborhood tavern, though some loyalists lament its move from dingier digs nearby, down the street from the **Old Town Ale House**. Full of character and characters, the charmingly dilapidated Old Town is a popular destination for cutups from nearby Second City and for other improvisers around town. (One cast of regulars, circa 1970, is memorialized in a fading mural.) You can barely see through the windows of this corner tavern, housed in a 19th-century building; the owner says she spends a lot of money "to keep it looking seedy." These two bars once formed the so-called Bermuda Triangle along with another favorite media haunt, the reporter's mecca **Billy Goat Tavern** on lower North Michigan Avenue. This dive deluxe still feels pretty authentic despite the onslaught of tourists, who flock here to see the "cheezeborga, cheezeborga" joint immortalized on "Saturday Night Live."

The college life... There are a multitude of bars on Lincoln Avenue, and it helps to have a gimmick to stand out from the pack. **Bamboo Bernies** has adopted a pseudo-Polynesian theme, with limbo contests, a sandlot volleyball court, and drinks like the "Shark Bite" (a 96-ounce vodka and lemonade concoction served in a fishbowl with a rubber shark). Par-tee! It's the same basic mood down the block at **The Big Nasty**, a teeming den of hooligans toting 22-ounce beers. Even on the coldest nights, a line of students in Big 10 sweatshirts and graduates holding down their first jobs stretches out the door at **Hi-Tops Cafe**, a hot spot in a renovated warehouse across from Wrigley Field. The big-screen TVs in the airy, raftered main room are tuned to "Melrose Place" on Mondays, where the barely drinking-age devotees of the Fox soap congregate.

Slacker scenes... Artists, rock god wannabes, and pierced-and-tattooed copy-shop employees have created their own exile community in the 'hoods of Wicker Park and Bucktown. Ground zero is **Rainbo Club**, a former private Polish social club with alternative cachet and a reputation as a hangout for touring indie rockers. Dating to 1936, the bar has a display case for art along the front wall and a small stage area where polka bands once performed. Today, bartenders (who've included members of cult fave Tortoise) spin rock records, and there's even a photo booth to accommodate tourists. On those nights when you're torn between staying in or going out, **Danny's Tavern** in Bucktown gives you the best of both worlds. Feeling social? Go no farther than the faux-fur covered stools at the busy front bar. Or in a cliquish way? Then disappear with your car-pool mates into one of the chambers in the back and chill on an old couch. In case you show up at **Urbis Orbis** without companionship or reading matter, check out one of the offbeat periodicals for sale or the exuberantly graffiti-covered unisex john, at least until the waify waitrons behind the big oval bar finally register your presence. Wicker Park's original coffeehouse hosts spoken-word, experimental music, and the occasional touring singer-songwriter in its spare theater space. The loafing vibe has been imported to the fringes of Lincoln Park at **Delilah's**, a dark, somewhat sinister bar with a lot of rock-'n'-roll attitude. The music matters here: Depending on the night, a DJ spins everything from country to punk and ska to lounge music, and customers have their say on the rock jukebox on weekends. Low-key but less adventurous is **Sheffield's Beer and Wine Garden**, a laid-back saloon where Lake View guys and gals show up in cutoffs. There's lots of room to spread out and a couple of elevated seating areas for surveying the scene. For a night of shooting pool and hanging with friends, arrive early at Lake View's **Ten Cat Tavern**, an unpretentious neighborhood spot, to claim the fifties-flavored back room warmed by a working fireplace. Smokers will appreciate the humongous ceramic ashtrays here.

Where the boys are... An evening stroll down a ten-block strip of North Halsted Street, the Main Street of the Lakeside gay enclave known as Boys Town, will keep any curious bar-crawler occupied late into the night. Evening excursions often embark from **Roscoe's Tavern and Cafe**, an inviting saloon populated by clean-cut, Gap-wearing guys that's within easy reach of the other bars in the area. A few laps around the loud, warmly lit front bar, a quick peek at the garden patio, and a tune or two on the dance floor, and you'll be ready to follow the stream of barflies dodging traffic across the street to **Sidetrack**, a supersleek video bar where the cute guy ogling you might actually be watching one of the ubiquitous video monitors above your head—a nonstop barrage of show tunes, comedy clips, and music videos. Just when the scene was getting a bit stale, **Cocktail** started mixing up martinis and the Cosmopolitans made famous at the owners' first night spot (see Espial). The retro theme doesn't extend beyond the drinks and Cary Grant flicks on the TV, though; the decor at this corner bar is generic trendy, the mood relatively muted and intimate. The fun jukebox is stocked with divas, disco, and the likes of Dean Martin. The oldest bar on the strip, **Little Jim's** has been around for two decades. It's a basic tavern, nothing fancy—a jukebox and porn videos on the tube will do. Despite its name, **Big Chicks** is a hangout for an arty crowd of gay men. But the place is far from homogeneous: Lesbians, straights, club kids, and neighborhood types are all thrown into the mix. Credit the Uptown location, which makes this effervescent, filled-to-the-gills bar a destination and not an afterthought. Among its virtues: cheap midnight shots, a high-camp jukebox, convivial staff, and owner Michelle Fire's funky personal art collection by and of (what else?) big chicks.

Java joints... Sophisticated and cosmopolitan, **The Third Coast on Delaware** is a bustling off-Michigan Avenue spot where lots of very well dressed, very good looking, European-sounding persons prop their elbows up on the tightly packed tables, with cigarettes hanging from their fingers; backgammon players occasionally interrupt a hotly contested game to place calls on cell phones. The high people-watching quotient gives this hip joint all the glamour of a bar. Before there were espresso bars at car washes and shoe stores in the city, there was **No Exit Cafe and Gallery**, the oldest coffeehouse in the Chicago area. Since it opened in 1958, it's had several owners and locations, and still draws Rogers Park activists, neo-Beats with laptops, and other locals for conversation and live folk and jazz to its down-to-earth location along the el tracks. Age-old wooden furniture and accumulated detritus like a stuffed armadillo, trophies, and a Beethoven bust furnish a no-frills room that's so intimate you're forced to pay attention when performers take the stage. Nearby is the terrifically idiosyncratic **Don's Coffee Club**, a storefront cafe with a homey feel. The owner (Don, natch) has decorated the place with mismatched furnishings; serves tea and coffee in old china cups and saucers; spins LPs by the likes of Glenn Miller, Josephine Baker, and Tommy Dorsey; and gabs with the regulars about soap operas and his favorite old movies (hence the house blend, Casablanca). The chalkboard menu lists coffee, tea, ginger ale, and food items like toasted cheese sandwiches, hot dogs, and proudly served store-bought cake, pie, and ice cream. The globe-trotting owners of **Kopi, A Traveler's Cafe** have played out the theme at their comfy Andersonville coffeehouse with travel books for sale, an ethnic clothing and handicrafts boutique, and clocks reporting the time from Kansas City to Kyoto. Patrons are invited to add info to a traveler's file of recommendations. Make sure you don't have any holes in your socks if you opt to sit at a table in the Eastern-style lounge area up front: Everybody sitting on one of the pillows has to take off their shoes. At **Urbis Orbis**, a cavernous coffeehouse in Wicker Park, a scruffy crowd of arty types, students, labor organizers, and other neighborhood folks all seem engrossed, debating the local art scene, making plans for the next newsletter, staring out the window onto North Avenue, pulling a drag on a hand-rolled cigarette. Numerous tiny revolutions are fomented here daily. Stationed near the city's other major bohemian crossroads of Belmont and Clark streets, **Scenes Coffeehouse and Dramatist Bookstore** is a cramped hangout for local kids, as well as aspiring playwrights and poets drawn to the shelves of theater-related volumes. Floor-to-ceiling windows accommodate the entertaining scenery on Clark Street. A few blocks away is the city's first cyber-cafe, **Interactive Bean**, which has been wired with a dozen or so Internet-linked Macs and video cameras for teleconferencing with cafe habitués on the coasts. The setup is pretty neat: You can relax on a couch and sip your coffee while pointing and clicking on one of the computers. But whether the cyber-cafe concept stays online in Chicago is still up for grabs—there's never a problem getting computer time here.

Notice what pervasive coffeehouse ingredient is missing from **Uncommon Ground**. Nobody's blowing smoke rings. That's right, the two-room coffeehouse located up the road from Wrigley Field is smoke free. On top of that, it's a cozy, comfortable spot with a fireplace when it's cold outside and outdoor seating when it's not.

Juke joints... Just about every bar in Chicago has a soulless new CD jukebox loaded with a million Pearl Jam tracks. A few purists, however, have retained old jukes which dispense 45rpm records or given special care to their musical repertoires. The Uptown gay bar **Big Chicks** is a true jukebox connoisseur's mecca, with not one but two jukes. There's a Space Age blue-and-pink machine dating to 1967 that allows you to watch records load up and spin, but it's only used on special occasions; the other's more modern, but still plays an eclectic and campy mix of 45s, from old standards to disco to cheesy rock and roll (remember Billy Squier?), on nights when there's not a DJ at work. For special events, the juke is spiced up with songs appropriate to the occasion, drawn from management's archive of 10,000 records (The Pretenders' "Back on the Chain Gang" and Devo's "Whip It" were added for International Mr. Leather weekend). Try Madonna's cover of "Fever," then head over to the **Green Mill Cocktail Lounge** for Peggy Lee's original. Kicking in between sets, the Green Mill's Galaxy 200, which glows like a hearth, is stocked with the kind of 45s you might expect from this jazz joint: heavy doses of Ella, Billie, and Frank (of course, "Chicago"), as well as Duke Ellington, Glenn Miller, and Marlene Dietrich. (See The Club Scene.) Jazz lovers also keep the juke at Bucktown's **Blue Note** busy with a huge number of jazz, blues, and soul CDs from the likes of Charlie Parker, Aretha Franklin, John Coltrane, Ray Charles, and Clarence "Gatemouth" Brown.

The records at **The Lodge** are as venerable as this snug and woodsy Division Street bar, spanning oldie favorites from the fifties to the seventies. Amplified through its own speakers, the 1958 Seeburg Select-o-Matic at **Hopleaf** in Andersonville doesn't play anything recorded later than the early sixties. You get two plays for a quarter (one of the best deals in town) from the R&B, gospel, hillbilly, and jazz offerings—stuff from Ricky Nelson, Sarah Vaughan, (early) Stevie Wonder, Jerry Lee Lewis, and Nathaniel Mayer & the Fabulous Twilights.

Hipper and more laid-back than most of the other bars in its vicinity, Lake View's **Ginger Man Tavern** has a jukebox that's heavy on roots rock, blues, soul, and R&B—songs by James Brown, Lee Dorsey ("Working in a Coal Mine"), Fats Domino, Freddy King, and Al Green. The totally fun oldies juke at Bucktown's **Marie's Riptide Lounge** is a big draw. The house favorite is "Hooked on a Feeling" by Blue Suede, but every song is a classic, no matter how schmaltzy. Here you'll find Chubby Checker, Bobby Darin ("Mack the Knife"), Engelburt Humperdinck, Ray Conniff, Ray Anthony ("The Hokey Pokey"), lots from the King, and a few by the Village People. And who can forget Jim Nabors' cover of "Impossible Dream"?

Elsewhere, you'll find punk and subversive rock like Jesus Lizard, Bad Brains, the Pixies, Kiss, Pavement, and the Velvet Underground at **Delilah's** in Lincoln Park; tons of disco, R&B, and lounge-core from Stevie Wonder, Earth, Wind & Fire, Esquivel, Eartha Kitt, and Bananarama at trendy **Espial**, also in Lincoln Park; and classic crooners like Edith Piaf, Rosemary Clooney, and Barbra Streisand at the seedy Old Town classic, the **Old Town Ale House**. At **The Ink Well**, just off Michigan Avenue, people actually boogie on the tiny dance floor next to the awesome jukebox (Stevie Wonder to the Stones). A recent graffito scrawled in the men's room summed up the affectionate attitude that regulars have for this bar: "The Well is the Center of All Creation."

Piano bars... A pianist at the **Seasons Lounge** in the Four Seasons Hotel, just off Michigan Avenue, supplies soft background music during the week; a jazz trio entertains on weekends. Sumptuously upholstered sofas and armchairs are scattered about, creating a wealth of options for settling in for the night. For years, pianist Buddy Charles has charmed a crowd of mostly out-of-towners and business travelers at **Coq d'Or** at the old-money Drake Hotel, anchoring the north end of Michigan Avenue.

Beer here... With a beer count that management claims tops 150 different microbrews, it's a shame that **House of Beer** is marooned on self-parodic Division Street, where bar-hoppers seem more interested in keeping their buzz going than in trying an unfamiliar bottle. The owners seem to acknowledge that everyone doesn't appreciate variety: They keep an iced tub of Lites just inside the door. The retro-sportsman look here is carried out with knotty-pine walls, waitrons donning khaki fishing vests, and random memorabilia on the walls, but it all gets lost in the sea of guys wearing J.Crew button-downs, smoking stogies, and downing exotic microbrews. It's one big frat party at the North Side's **Great Beer Palace**, where revelers pick from two dozen drafts; down six European beers at one sitting and you'll be rewarded with a plastic Viking helmet and your Polaroid mounted on the wall. Location scouts looking to film a Gen-X beer commercial need go no further than the Andersonville pub **Hopleaf**: Locals pushing 30 sit for hours in a few booths and on bentwood barstools drinking the neighborhood bar's fine menu of microbrews. Take a peek at the brewing equipment on your way into **Goose Island Brewing Company**, the city's original microbrewery. Vintage advertising signage provides a visual backdrop at this old brick warehouse engulfed by a sprawl of stores and parking lots. Goose Island features a fermented repertoire of 40 rotating brews, including its flagship Honker's Ale, a smooth brew which you'll also find on tap at many other bars around town. Outsider **Rock Bottom Brewery**, one of a Boulder, Colorado–based chain of brewpubs, serves a red ale, a stout, and three other kinds of beer made on the premises of its restaurant and bar in a nicely restored, if somewhat bland, River North building; while eating or drinking, you can peer onto the fermenting vessels. The rambling bar buzzes after work with a yuppie crowd cheering the Bulls, shooting pool, and sampling the home brew. Lincoln Park's English-style **John Barleycorn Memorial Pub** has an enormous beer garden and a covered patio area; inside are two high-ceilinged rooms decorated with vintage model sailing vessels and nautical-themed artwork. You'll feel like you're hanging out in a friend's backyard in the leafy beer garden at **Cody's Public House**, which even has its own outdoor bocci court and dart boards. This laid-back Lake View spot, named for its owner's mutt, has a beautiful vintage bar inside and a well-rounded mix of patrons hanging out. Also in Lake View, you'll find a brick beer garden canopied by an enormous tree at **Sheffield's Beer and Wine Garden** (as you'd guess from the name); it's one of the few places in

Chicago where you can shoot pool outside. The chalkboard menu at Sheffield's boasts 60-plus offerings, most of them regional microbrews. Trying not to overwhelm its postcollegiate regulars, the tavern guides your choice with one recommended and one "bad" beer of the month, as well as a free glossary of beer terms (from *aftertaste* to *wheat beer*).

Martini madness... These days, just about every bar in the city has latched onto the martini revival as a promotional gimmick; some have gone so far as to make it their signature drink. The front bar at the swank Bucktown diner **Club Lucky** (see Late Night Dining) is a jammed waiting area for the dining room on weekends, but come earlier in the week and it's a quiet place to sip the special house martini: vodka shaken, chilled, and served straight up with a blue-cheese-stuffed olive. They also do a black martini, adding a splash of Chambord to vodka. Check out the martinis at Lincoln Park's **Espial**, a joint so suave you'd expect Cary Grant to stroll in any minute; the fiery-red cocktail lounge in back is decorated with kitschy garage-sale finds and *Breakfast at Tiffany's* on the tube. The martinis are as big as the steaks at **Gibsons Bar & Steakhouse**, where they serve their namesake drink in a 10-ounce glass. The bartenders at this sleek Rush Street nightspot shake vodka or gin and just a spray of vermouth and top it off with a hand-stuffed olive (pimento, blue cheese, or anchovy).

Places to drink scotch... The biggest stash of single-malt scotch whiskey in the city is found at **Buckingham's**, a sleek bar and steakhouse downtown in the Chicago Hilton and Towers, where the glass liquor case is stocked with about 100 different kinds of scotch. A select few in the bar's scotch drinkers club have their names engraved on a plaque commemorating their successful sampling of the entire collection. Every other month or so, the bartender nervously pours out a snifter of $325-a-glass Glenfiddich Silver Stag, trying not to spill a single drop. The **Big Brasserie and Bar** at the Hyatt Regency downtown gets its name not only from its physical size but from the length of its drink list, including 40 different kinds of scotch. A little less intimidating is the down-home Lake View pub **The Duke of**

Perth, a Scottish-owned enterprise where the selection of single-malt scotches is equally impressive yet a bit less pricey. Drawing neighborhood folks and scotch connoisseurs, the cozy bar up front gives everyone the chance to enjoy an intimate dialogue with the bartender about what to try next.

Margaritaville... It's not surprising that one of the country's most lauded Mexican restaurants, **Frontera Grill**, mixes up several distinct margaritas in its small festive bar, including a strong (but so-so) premade Cuervo Gold margarita with a Spanish orange liqueur, a blue aguave variation with cointreau, and another with Oaxacan mezcal, brandy, and bitters. For a twist on things, try a margarita at **The Matchbox**, a tiny corner tavern in Ukrainian Village: The bartenders serve them straight up in a martini glass and top them off with lime, lemon peel, and a dusting of powdered sugar, not salt, around the rim. It sounds weird, but it's deelish. A giant sombrero marks the entrance to **El Jardín Cantina**, the bar adjunct to a Lake View Mexican restaurant, where the huge margaritas are infamous. Every Chicagoan recalls drinking one; two, they can't remember. The rumor that they're spiked with grain alcohol is just that, but these margaritas are indeed wicked, wicked things.

A wine list... If you're the type who picks wines by the pretty labels, **Webster's Wine Bar** may be more your speed. You can buy vino by the glass or train your palate by sampling flights of Merlot, Chardonnay, and Pinot Noir at the Lincoln Park wine bar, which provides place mats labeled with the names of each of the four or five samples. An odd assortment of chairs and tables are scattered about the dimly lit place; a library area in back, supplied with old books and encyclopedias, is given over to cigar smoking (you can get away from the smoke at the sidewalk cafe). The vibrant sidewalk cafe at **The Third Coast**, a block off Michigan Avenue, is the closest you'll get to Paris in Chicago, all the more so with one of a choice of two dozen bottles of wine. They're always ready for a special occasion at **Star Bar**: Attached to the elegant Lake View music room Pops for Champagne (see The Club Scene), it also stocks more than 125 kinds of sparkling wines.

After hours... After most of the city's bars turn off the lights and go home, thirsty, sleepless Chicagoans extend their evening by flocking to a few late-night spots. Word has spread beyond Bucktown about the Twilight Zone-ish charm of **Marie's Riptide Lounge**, a venerable bar taken over by denim-shirted twentysomethings when their nocturnal habitats in Lincoln Park close shop. After 2am, the line starts forming outside the **Blue Note**, a Bucktown bar popular with others in the bar biz. Everyone is cast in a cool blue light from the glass-brick bar area. The tatty, earthy charm of the amber-lit **Old Town Ale House** (in Old Town, natch) makes it a tempting last stop. Three pinball machines, a lending library (containing nothing you really want to read), Guinness on tap, and a wonderful jukebox help folks wind down for the night.

The Index

The standard closing time is 2am Sunday through Friday, 3am Saturday; we note below if any bars deviate from this.

Adagio. At this upscale bar and restaurant popular with the Lincoln Park jet set, you'll find live jazz or lite rock most nights downstairs, cocktail party chatter upstairs to a loud disco soundtrack. In summer, the garden patio is a pleasure.... *Tel 312/787–0400. 923 W. Weed St., Red Line North & Clybourn el stop. Closed Sun. $5–10 cover some nights.*

Bamboo Bernies. This gimmicky Lincoln Park bar courts the college crowd.... *Tel 773/549–3900. 2247 N. Lincoln Ave., Red Line Fullerton el stop. Closed Mon–Tues. Open until 4am.*

The Berghoff. The SRO bar at this ancient German restaurant serves up several of its own brews and carved roast beef sandwiches.... *Tel 312/427–3170. 17 W. Adams St., Red Line Jackson & State el stop. Open until 9pm.*

Big Brasserie and Bar. Views of the Michigan Avenue skyline, brews from an exhaustive drink list (especially cognacs and scotches).... *Tel 312/565–1234, Hyatt Regency Chicago, 151 E. Wacker Dr., Red Line Washington & State el stop.*

Big Chicks. An out-of-the-way gay alternative to the Halsted Street party parade, this popular two-room Uptown bar gets crowded (and *very* smoky) on weekends. Free Sunday afternoon buffets and a DJ spinning dance tunes on weekends.... *Tel 773/728–5511. 5024 N. Sheridan Rd., Red Line Argyle el stop.*

The Big Nasty. A spartan playroom, built for abuse, where post-college types get unapologetically drunk and messy. Upstairs there's a sports bar and dance floor.... *Tel 773/404–1535. 2242 N. Lincoln Ave., Red Line Fullerton el stop. Open Wed–Sat. $2 cover weekends.*

Billy Goat Tavern. Newspaper mementos of years past cover the walls of this favorite media hangout, located underneath the Wrigley Building.... *Tel 312/222–1525. 430 N. Michigan Ave., Red Line Grand & State el stop.*

Bluebird Lounge. At this dark, hip-yet-unpretentious bar, there's a good selection of regional microbrews on tap, pinball, and no TV!.... *Tel 312/642–3449. 1637 N. Clybourn Ave., Red Line North & Clybourn el stop.*

Blue Note. This long, two-room Bucktown bar, big on jazz and R&B, fills up after other bars have closed.... *Tel 773/489–0011. 1901 W. Armitage Ave., Blue Line Western el stop, then transfer to 73 Armitage bus. Open until 4am.*

Buckingham's. Clad in gray marble, this restaurant-bar in the Chicago Hilton and Towers is renowned for its selection of top-shelf scotch.... *Tel 312/922–4400, ext 6600. 720 S. Michigan Ave., Red Line Harrison & State el stop. Open until 11pm.*

Cactus Bar & Grill. Traders acclimated to frenzied yelling fests all day at work don't seem to mind the high-wattage sound system here at this south Loop southwest-themed party place.... *Tel 312/922–3830. 404 S. Wells St., Brown Line Van Buren & LaSalle el stop. Open until 10pm. Closed weekends.*

Cité. Mirrored piano bar on top of a condo, noteworthy mainly for its view.... *Tel 312/644–4050. 505 N. Lake Shore Dr., Red Line Grand el stop, then transfer to 29 State or 65 Grand bus. Open until 11pm Sun–Thur, 12am Fri–Sat.*

The Closet. Lesbians hang out at this unpretentious Lake View video bar, but gay men and straights mix here too. Monthly "Bang Yer Head" heavy-metal nights.... *Tel 773/477–8533. 3325 N. Broadway, Red Line Belmont el stop. Open until 4am.*

Cocktail. This latest gay neighborhood spot is well suited for conversation. If you're so inclined, sit inside the fishbowl-like facade to see if anyone's fishin'.... *Tel 773/477–1420. 3357 N. Halsted St., Red Line Belmont el stop.*

Cody's Public House. On a quiet Lake View residential street, this corner tavern offers distractions like darts, billiards, a jukebox, and board games.... *Tel 773/528–4050. 1658 W. Barry Ave., Brown Line Paulina el stop.*

Coq d'Or. Customers settle into the red Naughahyde banquettes or crowd around the keyboard at this cozy bar in the Drake Hotel.... *Tel 312/787–2200. 140 E. Walton St., Red Line Chicago & State el stop. Open until 2am, 1am Sun.*

Danny's Tavern. A couple of immense dogs sprawled in your path tip you off to the laid-back attitude at this Bucktown bar. Good beer selection, and the $2 Tuesday special is a local favorite.... *Tel 773/489–6457. 1951 W. Dickens St., Blue Line Damen el stop.*

Delilah's. Find your way to the bar and you'll have a choice of 50 beers and as many bourbons; follow the exposed electrical wiring upstairs for pinball and pool. On Saturdays, the Psychotronic Film Society screens locally produced indie films.... *Tel 773/472–2771. 2771 N. Lincoln Ave., Brown Line Diversey el stop.*

Don's Coffee Club. In contrast to the rough strip outside, this quirky Rogers Park coffeehouse is bathed in the glow of kitschy table lamps and brightened further by cheesy seventies beach-scene wallpaper. On Sunday nights in summer, people dance to swing tunes on the patio.... *Tel 773/274–1228. 1439 W. Jarvis Ave., Red Line Jarvis el stop. Open until 1am Sun–Wed, 2am (or later) weekends. Closed Thur.*

The Duke of Perth. This warm neighborhood spot is really a Scottish pub dressed up with all kinds of antique clocks, photos, and such. Dinner menu and wide selection of single-malt scotches.... *Tel 773/477–1741. 2913 N. Clark St., Red Line Belmont el stop. Open until 2am, 1am Mon.*

El Jardín Cantina. This Lake View attraction has 'em lined up out the door for the potent margaritas. There's a dance floor upstairs and a cafe and restaurant a block or so south.... *Tel 773/327–4646. 3401 N. Clark St., Red Line Addison el stop. Closed Sun–Mon.*

Espial. This hep cocktail lounge is attached to a Lincoln Park bistro where straight and gay swingers sip the house specialty, Cosmopolitans, and enjoy quiet conversation.... *Tel 773/871–8123. 948 W. Armitage Ave., Brown Line Armitage el stop. Open until midnight Sun–Wed, 2am Thur–Fri, 3am Sat.*

Frontera Grill. At this acclaimed River North Mexican restaurant, bartenders will mix up a few of the margarita specialties for you, all prepared with fresh lime juice.... *Tel 312/661–1434. 445 N. Clark St., Brown Line Merchandise Mart el stop. Open until 10pm Tues–Thur, 11pm weekends. Closed Sun–Mon.*

Gamekeepers. Television monitors never leave your field of vision at this Lincoln Park sports bar. Kitchen snacks until midnight.... *Tel 773/549–0400. 345 W. Armitage Ave., Brown Armitage el stop. Open until 4am. Occasional cover for bands.*

Get Me High Lounge. Set on a neighborhood block, this tiny Bucktown dive is oddly romantic, with low, low ceilings and candlelight.... *Tel 773/252–4090. 1758 N. Honore St., Blue Line Damen el stop.*

Gibsons Bar and Steakhouse. Status symbol cars at the valet stand tip you off to the high-powered schmoozing, boozing, and cruising inside this Gold Coast hot spot.... *Tel 312/266–8999. 1028 N. Rush St., Red Line Chicago & State el stop. Open until 2am (earlier on weeknights).*

Ginger Man Tavern. This unpretentious Wrigleyville bar offers a nice alternative to its frenzied sports bar environs. A huge selection of microbrews on tap and a pool table in the back room.... *Tel 773/549–2050. 3740 N. Clark St., Red Line Addison el stop.*

Goose Island Brewing Company. This brewpub-restaurant on the south end of Lincoln Park has a handsome rectangular front bar. Making plans to open a second location at its West Side microbrewery.... *Tel 312/915–0071. 1800 N.*

Clybourn Ave., Red Line North & Clybourn el stop. Open until 1am Sun–Thur, 2am weekends.

The Great Beer Palace. The digs are far from palatial, but the bar sure is great, with two dozen beers on tap.... *Tel 773/525–4906. 4128 N. Lincoln Ave., Brown Line Irving Park el stop. Open until 1am weeknights, 2am Fri, 3am Sat.*

Green Orchid Room. The olive-hued deco bar at the downtown Bismarck Hotel is a fine place to settle into a booth and sip a martini.... *Tel 312/236–0123. 171 W. Randolph St., Brown Line Wells & Randolph el stop. Open until midnight Tues–Thur, 1am Fri–Sat. Closed Sun–Mon.*

Guthrie's Tavern. A casual Wrigleyville neighborhood bar, crowded on weekends.... *Tel 312/477–2900. 1300 W. Addison St. Red Line Addison el stop. Open until 4am.*

Hana Lounge. This urbane lobby bar is an intimate setting for cocktails and conversation, with jazz every night (except Sunday). A new sake bar features two dozen varieties.... *Tel 312/744–1900. Hotel Nikko, 320 N. Dearborn St., Red Line Grand & State el stop. Open until 1am.*

Hi-Tops Cafe. A renovated warehouse within the shadow of Wrigley Field, this ridiculously popular saloon hosts a college sweatshirt-wearing crowd. Technically a restaurant, Hi-Tops serves burgers, wings, and other stuff until closing.... *Tel 773/348–0009. 3551 N. Sheffield Ave., Red Line Addison el stop. $3–5 occasional cover.*

Hopleaf. The North Side Andersonville neighborhood is served well by this low-key barroom, a meeting place for young and hip newcomers to this old-time Swedish part of town.... *Tel 773/334–9851. 5148 N. Clark St., Red Line Berwyn el stop or 22 Clark St. bus.*

House of Beer. This Rush Street area theme bar serves lots of exotic beers. A good place for a pitcher.... *Tel 312/642–2344. 16 W. Division St., Red Line Clark & Division el stop. Open until 4am.*

Howard's Bar and Grill. There's a fireplace in winter, a patio in summer, at this denlike bar a block off North Michigan

Avenue. Jukebox and good bar food until midnight.... *Tel 312/787-5269. 152 E. Ontario St., Red Line Grand & State el stop. Open until 2am Mon–Fri, 3am Sat, 7pm Sun.*

The Hunt Club. This multilevel Rush Street bar includes a raised cigar lounge overlooking the small dance floor and a sunken pool room.... *Tel 312/988-7887. 1100 N. State St., Red Line Chicago & State el stop. Open until 4am.*

Icon Bar & Cafe. This lesbian cocktail lounge in River North attracts an after-work crowd; later, lots of couples stop in to sample a late-night menu of salads and ethnic appetizers. Latinas show up for salsa nights on Wednesdays and Fridays.... *Tel 312/649-1192. 710 N. Clark St., Red Line Chicago & State el stop.*

The Ink Well. At this totally untrendy subterranean hangout just off Michigan Avenue, everybody knows everybody, they all drink martinis (there's no tap), and they're here so much that they get phone calls.... *Tel 312/944-8232. 226 E. Ontario St., Red Line Grand & State el stop. Closed Sun.*

Interactive Bean. This spiffy Lake View coffee bar was the first in the city dedicated to cruising the Internet.... *Tel 773/528-2881. 1137 W. Belmont Ave., Red Line Belmont el stop. Open until 11:30pm Sun–Thur, 1am Fri–Sat.*

Jesse Livermore's. A clubby, refined downtown lounge named after the high-rolling New York trader of the twenties, it has an excellent beer and wine selection and four different kinds of martini.... *Tel 312/786-5272. 401 S. LaSalle St., Brown Line Van Buren & LaSalle el stop. Open until midnight. Closed weekends.*

Jimmy's Woodlawn Tap. A gritty University of Chicago hangout for smoking, drinking, and pontificating.... *Tel 773/643-5516. 1172 E. 55th St., Dan Ryan line Garfield el stop.*

John Barleycorn Memorial Pub. This handsome antique bar is great for quiet conversation, with piped-in classical music, three dozen beers on tap, a late-night kitchen, and a spacious outdoor patio.... *Tel 773/348-8899. 658 W. Belden St., Red Line Fullerton el stop.*

Kitty O'Shea's. A handsome, woodsy hotel pub where traditional Irish duos and trios perform nightly.... *Tel 312/922–4400, ext 4454. 720 S. Michigan Ave. (Chicago Hilton), Red Line Harrison & State el stop. Open until 1:30am.*

Kopi, A Traveler's Cafe. Named for the Indonesian word for coffee, this comfy Andersonville coffeehouse has arty tables and plants in the window. Live music a couple nights a week and daily international specials on the menu.... *Tel 773/989–5674. 5317 N. Clark St., Red Line Berwyn el stop or 22 Clark St. bus. Open until 11pm Sun–Thur, midnight weekends.*

Little Jim's. This pioneering Halsted Street gay bar still attracts a diverse clientele of all ages, races, and economic levels for some heavy cruising.... *Tel 773/871–6116. 3501 N. Halsted St., Red Line Addison el stop. Open until 4am.*

The Lodge. The smallest bar on this Division Street block exudes a cozy feel with antique paintings on the wall, oldies tunes in the air, and peanut dustings on the floor.... *Tel 312/642–4406. 21 W. Division St., Red Line Clark & Division el stop. Open until 4am.*

Marie's Riptide Lounge. This Bucktown late-night favorite has a long bar embellished with lava lamps, booths up front, and a funky little room in the back. Classic 45s on the jukebox.... *Tel 773/278–7317. 1745 W. Armitage Ave., 73 Armitage bus. Open until 4am.* Closed Mon.

The Matchbox. Located in an urban no-man's land, this tiny and aptly named bar was once a dive, but recently charmed up with art and candles and a finely stocked bar. Promise not to tell anyone else about it.... *Tel 312/666–9292. 770 N. Milwaukee Ave., Blue Line Chicago el stop.*

Melvin B's. A place that lives for the summer. The energetic sidewalk cafe is a major Rush Street scene. *Tel 312/751–9897. 1114 N. State Pkwy. Red Line Clark & Division el stop.*

Monk's Pub. A downtown hideaway, this pub has a weathered charm and a crazy big-city mix of customers. Good import beer list, standout burgers and chili, and a widescreen TV.... *Tel 312/357–6665. 203 W. Lake St., Red Line Randolph &*

Wells el stop. Open until midnight Mon–Thurs, 2am Fri. Closed weekends.

Mother's. Good times dance floor, blond bartenders in tight tops, and a gift shop, this relic of the singles scene still packs in the acid-washed masses.... *Tel 312/642–7251. 26 W. Division St., Red Line Clark & Division el stop. Open until 4am.*

No Exit Cafe and Gallery. This Rogers Park institution features a long list of coffees (a bottomless cup will run you $2.25), teas, hot chocolates, and iced coffees, as well as cafe chow.... *Tel 773/743–3355. 6970 N. Glenwood Ave., Red Line Morse el stop. Open until midnight Sun–Thur, 1am weekends. Closed Mon. Avg. $3 cover.*

Off the Line. A mostly lesbian neighborhood spot with a jukebox, darts, and a dry-eraser board depicting an ever-changing comic strip of same-sex couples.... *Tel 773/528–3253. 1829 W. Montrose Ave., Brown Line Montrose el stop.*

Old Town Ale House. An Old Town institution, this beat-up old saloon has a couple of cozy platformed nooks in the windows, but it's a lot more fun to sit at the bar and kibitz with everybody.... *Tel 312/944–7020. 219 W. North Ave., Brown Line Sedgwick el stop. Open until 4am.*

O'Rourke's. An intimate room with great wooden booths, this Lincoln Park tavern is conveniently located for après-theater, near both the Steppenwolf and the Royal George.... *Tel 312/335–1806, 1625 N. Halsted St., Red Line North & Clybourn el stop. Open until 2am.*

The Other Side. A North Side lesbian neighborhood tavern with a great location, across the street from a 24-hour bowling alley and a fast-food joint.... *Tel 312/404–8156. 3655 N. Western Ave., Brown Line Addison el stop. Closed Mon.*

P.J. Clarke's. With cigars for sale and a pretty good beer and wine list, the old-timey-looking place fills up with a good-looking crowd of tourists and local singles.... *Tel 312/664–1650. 1204 N. State Pkwy., Red Line Clark & Division el stop. Open until 2am every night.*

The Pump Room. The lively bar at this storied Chicago restaurant is ringed by romantic little cocktail tables. Nightly live music, tiny dance floor, steep drink prices.... *Tel 312/266–0360. Omni Ambassador East Hotel, 1301 N. State St., Red Line Chicago & State el stop. Open until 1am Sun–Thur, 2am weekends.*

Rainbo Club. This Wicker Park hangout hosts art students and slumming yuppies. Sink into one of the clubby booths or huddle around the circular bar.... *Tel 312/489–5999. 1150 N. Damen Ave., Blue Line Damen el stop.*

The Red Lion Pub. British beer and cider on tap and a large garden terrace in Lincoln Park. Regulars gather for Three Stooges and Marx Brothers flicks on Sundays.... *Tel 773/348–2695. 2446 N. Lincoln Ave., Red Line Fullerton el stop.*

Rock Bottom Brewery. Casual dining room on one side, spacious bar area on the other, this tasteful new downtown brewpub still feels kind of bland and suburban (e.g., there's a gift shop).... *Tel 312/755–9339. 1 W. Grand Ave., Red Line Grand & State el stop.*

Roscoe's Tavern and Cafe. There's something for everyone at this Boys Town gay bar: antique-filled front room dominated by a flowing bar, a billiard area, a dark dance floor in back, and an attached cafe.... *Tel 773/281–3355. 3356 N. Halsted St., Red Line Belmont el stop. $2 cover Sat.*

Scenes Coffeehouse and Dramatist Bookstore. At this Lake View cafe, two walls are lined with theater-related texts, from scripts to film history, and local auditions are posted.... *Tel 773/525–1007. 3168 N. Clark St., Red Line Belmont el stop. Open until 11:30pm Mon–Thur, 2:30am weekends.*

Schaller's Pump. Southsiders and Sox fans descend on the place to pick from a menu of burgers and steaks (and a corned beef and cabbage special on Thursdays).... *Tel 312/847–9378. 3714 S. Halsted St., Blue Line 35th St. el stop.*

Schulien's Restaurant and Saloon. First opened in 1886, this family-run Chicago institution is laden with memorabilia.... *Tel 312/478–2100. 2100 W. Irving Park Rd., Brown Line Irving Park el stop. Open until midnight. Usually. Closed Mon.*

Seasons Lounge. A restful oasis on the seventh floor of the Four Seasons Hotel on upper Michigan Avenue, the bar has a huge fireplace, bubbling fountains, and superplush furnishings. There's also a paneled English study for cigar chomping.... *Tel 312/280–8800. 120 Delaware Place, Red Line Chicago & State el stop. Open until 1am Mon–Fri, 2am Sat, midnight Sun.*

Sheffield's Beer and Wine Garden. It doesn't look like much from the street, but this Lake View corner tavern has depth: an array of rooms, a popular beer garden, and a beer selection worthy of the grand dark-wood bar.... *Tel 773/281–4989. 3258 N. Sheffield Ave., Red Line Belmont el stop. $1 cover weekends for beer garden.*

Sidetrack. This high-tech gay bar baby-sits some of the city's best-looking men with video clips of Barbra, Broadway, and "Ab Fab." All handsome wood and sexy stainless steel.... *Tel 773/477–9189. 3349 N. Halsted St., Red Line Belmont el stop.*

Signature Lounge. The trappings of this cocktail lounge on the 96th floor of the John Hancock Center aren't much better than a bland hotel lobby, but you're really here for the panoramic views. Live jazz during the week.... *Tel 312/787–7230. 875 N. Michigan Ave., Red Line Chicago & State el stop. Open until 1am Sun–Thur, 2am weekends.*

Sluggers. Big and boisterous, the biggest sports bar in Wrigleyville offers drink, food, sports TV, music, and games, both electronic and non.... *Tel 773/248–0055. 3540 N. Clark St., Red Line Addison el stop.*

Stanley's Kitchen & Tap. This lively neighborhood hot spot for Lincoln Park youngsters boasts a vast selection of bourbons.... *Tel 773/642–0007. 1970 N. Lincoln Ave., Brown Line Armitage el stop.*

Star Bar. A classy, comfortable Lake View bar with the same extensive champagne offerings as Pops for Champagne, the adjoining upscale jazz club.... *Tel 773/472–7272. 2934 N. Sheffield Ave., Red Line Belmont el stop.*

Ten Cat Tavern. Named in honor of the owners' multiple felines, this favorite neighborhood bar has a strong beer selection, pool tables, pinball, blues and roots-rock juke, and a backyard patio.... *Tel 773/935–5377. 3931 N. Ashland Ave., Brown Line Irving Park el stop.*

The Third Coast on Delaware. This popular neighborhood hangout for Gold Coasters serves coffee and a tasty menu of gourmet pizzas and salads. Outdoor seating expands this see-and-be-seen scene in good weather.... *Tel 312/664–7225. 29 E. Delaware Place, Red Line Clark & Division el stop.*

Uncommon Ground. A calming contrast to the club-hopping on Clark Street, this congenial neighborhood coffeehouse books local folk and blues artists and even puts out its own CD compilation. Nice sidewalk cafe for grazing on the large breakfast and dinner menu.... *Tel 773/929–3680. 1214 W. Grace St., Red Line Addison el stop. Open until 11pm, midnight in summer.*

Urbis Orbis. This high-ceilinged Wicker Park haven is a beehive of activity where you can linger for hours on end. Espresso drinks and a menu of salads, breads, and sandwiches (including a tofu melt).... *Tel 312/252–4446. 1934 W. North Ave., Blue Line Damen el stop. Open until midnight Sun–Thur, 1am weekends.*

Webster's Wine Bar. In a casual Lincoln Park bar, wine connoisseurs and neophytes alike can choose from more than 40 varieties of wine by the glass. Appetizer menu and jazz a couple nights a week.... *Tel 773/868–0608. 1480 W. Webster Ave., Brown Line Armitage el stop.*

Weeds. This candlelit Near North place with its funky-psychedelic decor features live rock and jazz and a big Monday poetry event. The combative owner/bartender is depicted in a plaster sculpture hoisting a bottle of Cuervo.... *Tel 312/943–7815. 1555 N. Dayton St., Red Line North & Clybourn el stop.*

Zak's. Dumpy enough to attract artists and other local Wicker Park boozers and keep others away.... *Tel 312/235–9063. 1443 N. Elk Grove Ave., Blue Line Damen el stop.*

the

3

arts

If not for Sir Georg Solti and David Mamet, Chicago may well have remained best known in the world of performing arts as the first stop for Broadway road shows.

Sure, there was the quietly fraying nightclub satire of Second City, the musty grandeur of the Lyric Opera and the Chicago Symphony Orchestra, but until Mamet and Solti made homes for themselves here, most creative types spent more energy trying to get out of here than creating new works. Then Sir Georg turned the CSO into an orchestra all the world envied (and Chicago lives to be envied), and Mamet, John Malkovich, Gary Sinise, and others in the Steppenwolf Theatre began giving a new voice to the American stage. Suddenly Chicago was on the world's cultural map for more than Hugh Hefner and "Kup's Show." And the city remains grateful.

It's a place to learn a craft. To hone skills. To develop your voice. Here you can start a theater company—people do it so often it's a bit of a cliché—put on a show in some rented basement and see who turns up. You can do it in Chicago—rents are pretty forgiving here. The stock of creative folk is constantly renewed by students coming out of the universities and emigrants from all over the Midwest, and once they've made a name for themselves here not everybody immediately jets off to the coasts anymore (and even when they do, they can't help but keep one finger in Chicago). Plenty of actors, musicians, and dancers, like regular nonartistic newcomers, find it such a manageable place to live that they end up staying. And that makes your job, as a connoisseur, all the harder on Saturday night—now you've got to choose from agate-size listings in the paper.

The big Broadway imports still roll into town and still quickly sell out, often running for months (at ever escalating prices) in downtown theaters like Adler and Sullivan's masterpiece Auditorium Theatre and the refurbished Chicago Theatre—recently taken over by Disney as a port of call for its splashy road shows. In another year or so another historic downtown movie palace, the Oriental Theatre, dormant and marqueeless for so long that a lot of people didn't even know it still existed, will reopen as a grand venue for big shows. But Chicagoans don't have to hold their breath for out of towners to give them a dose of cultchuh: The city hosts enough homegrown shows to keep more than 100 theater companies busy. And a few of them, like Steppenwolf and a few off-Loop theaters, have tested the waters in New York with hometown smashes—sometimes they've picked up a handful of Tony nominations or *New York Times* plaudits (Chicagoans *love* that). They've also returned home all wet. In some ways, theaters have replaced bars as a late-night alternative: Many of the more irreverent off-Loop theaters push curtain call back to 10:30pm (and even later), and some even allow alcoholic beverages, if they don't happen to sell it themselves. Even if more mature audiences can keep their eyes open that late, they might not want to, given the rawness of some of the themes. The city is also a magnet for young improv artists who want to show how quick witted they are; the comedy pipeline at Second City, though under repair after years of long and heavy use, is the main current of the scene. (One upstart theater company even did a whole show about their resentment of it.)

Sources

The city's main alternative paper, the ***Reader***, gets much of its heft from voluminous reviews, listings, and advertisements for concerts and performing arts. Published on Thursdays, the tabloid prides itself on providing the most complete theater coverage in the city, reviewing even the most obscure productions. More extensive profiles and analyses are carried in the ***Chicago Tribune***'s daily Arts section and its "Friday" entertainment pullout. The competing ***SunTimes*** isn't mandatory reading, but it's worth a look at its Friday "Weekend Plus" and Sunday "Showcase" sections. Look to the entertainment pullout section in ***N'Digo***, a free bimonthly tabloid, for an African-American perspective; ***¡Exito!*** is a Spanish-language free weekly that offers a calendar of events of Latino-related events; and the city's predominant lesbian and gay newspaper, ***Windy City Times***, offers its own spin on both gay and straight events. Tune into **WBEZ** (91.5 FM), the local National Public Radio affiliate, for erudite discussions of the latest happenings, during arts programs aired Friday and Saturday afternoons; and there's always the great, gray classical station **WFMT** (98.7 FM).

Getting Tickets

We're not sure what bothers us more about **Ticketmaster**: the teeth-gnashing service charges or the way the telephone reps repeat the logistics of your event ad nauseum. But if you're looking for tickets to concerts, Broadway imports, or sporting events, the monolithic ticket agent is still the only game in town. You can charge tickets on a credit card by calling 312/559-1212, or pay with cash only at one of their outlets at **Carson's Pirie Scott & Co.** (1 S. State St.), **Tower Records** (2301 N. Clark St.), or the three **Hot Tix** locations (see below). If you're willing to pay even bigger bucks, you can get tickets to just about any event by thumbing through the yellow pages for one of more than forty ticket brokers (all must be licensed by the state). Two reputable ones are **Tower Ticket Services** (tel 312/454-1300) and **Gold Coast Tickets** (tel 312/644-6446). They take credit card orders by phone and deliver overnight or the same day (of course, adding various commissions based on availability, demand, etc.). **Hot Tix** (tel 312/977-1755), run by the nonprofit League of Chicago Theaters, also sells half-price, day-of-show tickets to many theatrical productions, concerts, and dance performancees in the city and suburbs. Available by credit card, check, or cash, tickets can be purchased in person at one of three locations: the sixth level of the **Chicago Place** mall (700 N. Michigan Ave.); across from Marshall Field's in the Loop (108 N. State St.); and at the **City Parking Garage** in Evanston (1616 Sherman Ave.). Getting there early always helps ensure that you get to choose from the widest selection of shows; ticket availability varies from day to day, but most don't sell out until later in the day. The outlets are open daily, and tickets to many Sunday performances are sold on Saturday. Larger theaters guarantee seats by using plastic over the phone, though you might want to save on the minimal service charge by stopping by the box office. A few theaters, including the biggest ones in town, offer discount or half-price tickets at the box office the night of the performance. Many others regularly reduce the price of admission for students and seniors.

Last-Minute Discount Deals

Above and beyond the ticket sources outlined in Down and Dirty, here are a few insider tips for snaring cheap seats. You can snap up half-price tickets to the Steppenwolf Theatre Company by calling or stopping by the box office after 5pm on the night of a performance. The Goodman Theatre's "Tix by Six" scheme offers half-price, day-of-performance tickets: Extra tickets (often excellent, turned-back subscription passes) go on sale at 1pm for matinees, 6pm for evening shows. Rarely is anyone turned away. **Lookingglass Theatre Company** also offers a limited number of $10 tickets before performances. Even when the **Chicago Symphony Orchestra**'s concerts are sold out, turned-back tickets from subscribers are often available the night of the performance. The **Lyric Opera of Chicago** also regularly sells out long in advance, but check with the box office for turned-back tickets in advance or the day of a performance.

The Lowdown

The theater establishment... Every year, scads of earnest young theater grads dream of following the trajectory of the highly regarded **Steppenwolf Theatre Company**, which was born out of a North Shore church basement in the seventies and has settled down into a state-of-the art theater complex in Lincoln Park. These perpetrators of the "in your face" Chicago acting school recently faced a midlife crisis of sorts, with many of its founding members long gone from Chicago and preoccupied with projects in New York and Hollywood. After a few local duds and mixed results from its forays onto Broadway (years after its *The Grapes of Wrath* took home two Tonys), a new board has used the star power of the ensemble (John Malkovich, Gary Sinise, et al.) and a few young Hollywood turks (Ethan Hawke, Martha Plimpton) to restore its luster. Things look pretty good: A revival of Sam Shepard's *Buried Child,* directed by Sinise, went on to Broadway and a handful of Tony nominations.

The other biggie in town is the **Goodman Theatre**, the city's oldest and largest resident theater, which offers a season of crowd-pleasing plays and musicals—often premieres by the likes of writers David Mamet and Edward Albee and director Frank Galati—with edgier works in its smaller studio theater.

Down in brainy Hyde Park, another of the city's venerable resident companies, the **Court Theatre**, presents classical drama, past and present, in its intimate 250-seat house. This well-established Actors Equity Theater started out decades ago as a group of teachers with a thing for Molière, and it keeps on expanding its literary scope. In recent seasons, it has very successfully staged two plays in repertory (Molière's *The Misanthrope* and Tom Stoppard's *Travesties*). No modern updates, no overly creative casting, just straight-ahead Shakespeare is what you get from **Shakespeare Repertory**, a respected company that mounts three solid productions each year, with both local actors and out-of-town guests, in a downtown theater, plus a popular freebie at the end of the summer in Grant Park. In Lincoln Park, **Victory Gardens** prides itself on premiering original Chicago plays and puts on good, if somewhat middlebrow, fare—the kind of stuff sure not to alienate people looking for a palatable dinner and a show.

Where to see Broadway shows... Splashy shows trucking into town put up their tents at a few of the city's grand old downtown theaters: the **Auditorium Theatre**, an Adler and Sullivan–designed architectural gem (originally home to the Chicago Symphony and the Lyric Opera, with wonderful acoustics) where musicals go for weeks and months on end; the **Shubert Theatre**, a 1906 vaudeville house that also hosts a lot of dance performances; and a refurbished 1921 movie palace, the **Chicago Theatre**, which recently was leased by Disney as a home for *Beauty and the Beast* and other cross-promotional theatrical fare. One of the biggest stories on the theater front in 1996 was the news that a producer plans to restore the Oriental Theatre to its former glory. When it reopens as a performing arts center right around the corner from the Chicago Theatre, in a year or so, this grande dame will provide another home for traveling shows.

If you need a reminder that they just don't build them like they used to, head out to the burbs, to the new $35 million **Rosemont Theatre**, a 4,000-plus-seat theater that it's doubtful anyone would want to restore decades from now. The gigantic lobby has a monstrous chandelier and dizzying M.C. Escher–like patterned carpet of comedy and tragedy masks; inside the theater, acoustics and sight lines are fine, but it looks like a multiplex cinema—the only things missing are cup holders on the seat arms. Adding insult to injury, Barry Manilow christened the place. The Rosemont hosts a Broadway subscription series of surefire winners like *Cats* and *Carousel.*

Small dramatic venues... Plenty of nomadic theater groups wander the city from storefront theaters to black-box beehives. One of the busiest spaces is Lincoln Park's **Royal George Theatre Center**. Here you'll find excellent productions, like *Angels in America,* in a comfortable and intimate 450-seat main-stage space or the crowd-pleasing barbershop revue *Forever Plaid* in the smaller cabaret. In Lake View, the **Theatre Building** has long nurtured fledgling thespian efforts of widely varying quality (even Steppenwolf debuted here way back when) in its three spaces connected to a busy lobby where everyone mingles. Shows sometimes gravitate here after finding audiences in smaller houses around town.

In Pilsen, one of the city's primary Mexican neighborhoods, the **Mexican Fine Arts Center Museum** has a handsome gallery that doubles as a performance space. It stages local theatrical productions and musical performances, both traditional and forward thinking. One of the newest small venues, Lake View's **Mercury Theater**, added its marquee to a street already lit up by the vintage Music Box Theater movie theater. It's a cozy and charming place—the exposed-brick walls are enhanced with a pair of stone Victorianesque busts—but since the debut production in 1996 bombed, the theater has been dark too many nights. The usual summer-stock fare has been ratcheted up a notch at the **Theatre on the Lake**, a Prairie Style building with the waves of Lake Michigan lapping practically at its door. More than half a dozen diverse groups now stage short runs of new and remounted productions here; unfortunately, it doesn't exactly have the poshest seating (folding chairs—ouch!).

On the fringes... The Chicago theater scene really came alive during the eighties—you can hardly walk a block on the North Side without stumbling across a plucky storefront theater. On any given night, a small production is guaranteed an audience of, say, seven or eight people, probably half of whom are related to the actors. Though some of the stuff can be raw or amateurish, a few original, exciting shows toil for months in modest, out-of-the-way theaters until a word-of-mouth buzz vaults the show onto a higher profile stage. Among the next generation, **Lookingglass Theatre Company**, an ensemble of handsome twentysomething Northwestern theater grads, has earned its media-darling status with highly physical, lyrically staged productions of literary works, as well as original plays rooted in company members' personal obsessions. They even have a certified star in their founding ranks: sensitive guy David Schwimmer, who, since reaching stardom on the TV series "Friends," has been pouring his new riches into the troupe (and putting all of his real-life Friends in his directorial film debut). One of the city's hottest young directors, Mary Zimmerman, is also an ensemble member. Another younger crew of NU grads, **Roadworks Productions**, got raves with the Midwestern premiere of Eric Bogosian's *subUrbia* and have followed it up with a few ambitious yet uneven presentations. They're a work-in-progress worth keeping an eye on.

In Lake View, **Bailiwick Repertory** is a busy theater center that's had its share of picks and pans, but it has always stretched itself with adventurous, creative productions (an adaptation of *Our Town* for the hearing impaired was one of last season's noteworthy offerings) and a venturesome annual gay-pride series. Wicker Park is home to a number of small spaces, among them the converted firehouse where **Latino Chicago Theater Company** plays to arty theater folk rather than the local Latino community, with a provocative repertoire emphasizing Nuyorican playwrights. They toss a few Spanish phrasings into the English texts of plays by Latin writers, along with making overtures to magical realism. It's a hike down to 75th Street for the city's most prominent African-American theater, the 25-year-old **ETA Creative Arts Foundation**, well respected for its top-flight staging of original or seldom-performed dramas by black playwrights from Chicago and elsewhere.

Late-night theater... Tired of Hollywood's pillaging of old TV shows? Blame the scandalous improvisers at **Annoyance Theatre**, who still haven't lived up to (or lived down) the runaway success of their *The Real Live Brady Bunch* a few years back. One of our favorite things about this Wrigleyville theater is its goofy show names (*Shake, Shake, Shake, Shake, Shake, Shake, Shake Your Ass*, or the after-midnight improv show *Screw Puppies*). They claim the city's longest-running musical, *Coed Prison Sluts*, a sophomoric parody of jailhouse films featuring a character who's introduced as being "just like Annie, except she's in prison and she's a whore." The show is chockful of anal-sex jokes and other naughty pranks guaranteed to get the frat boys in the audience laughing. Going to a performance here is akin to sitting in the bleachers at Wrigley Field down the street: You can smoke, drink (it's BYOB), and otherwise misbehave without disturbing the so-called actors on stage.

Overly sensitive types will also definitely want to steer clear of the way-out-there **Torso Theater**, a Lake View theater with a couple of hits—*Cannibal Cheerleaders on Crack* and *Shannen Doherty Shoots a Porno*—that have actually been running for years. It's a mixed bag at nearby **Cafe Voltaire**, a vegetarian eatery that draws amateur playwrights and performers—basically anybody who thinks it'd be neat to write or direct a play—out of the woodwork to try out their stuff in a subterranean theater furnished with crummy thrift-store couches. There's something for everyone in the nocturnal hit *Too Much Light Makes the Baby Go Blind,* performed by the Andersonville group **Neo-Futurists**. They promise "30 plays in 60 minutes," an entertaining evening (Friday or Saturday at 11:30pm) with much left to chance: Audience members pay $3 plus the roll of a six-sided die (therefore, $4–9) and determine the random order of short skits by shouting out their assigned numbers to performers. The group has written more than 2,000 plays, so no evening is ever the same. Get there early because it often sells out; while waiting, you can peruse the Hall of Presidents, a gallery of funky presidential portraits by local artists.

Improv... Improvisational comedy has spawned a bit of a cottage industry in Chicago. Young kids whose friends always tell them how funny they are load up their cars and head to Chicago to take improv classes, hoping maybe they'll end up on "Saturday Night Live." Of course, tourist magnet **The Second City** still looms large over the bustling scene, with its comedy revues skewering local politics and pop culture, capped each night by improvised sketches. The show's format—sketch, blackout, sketch—had gone stale in recent years, until the company shook things up by hiring away some of the city's best improvisers and borrowing a few tricks from other improv groups. The last few revues have come out winners. In Wrigleyville, **ImprovOlympic** has energized the improv scene with its student teams of sometimes very funny, sometimes insufferable, fresh-faced twentysomethings who invent loosely themed full-length pieces from individual audience suggestions. Enterprising graduates of the group often turn up with their own spin-off projects at **Cafe Voltaire**'s basement space and **Annoyance Theatre**. Another group taking up the long form is **The Free Associates**, an ensemble with a tiny Lakeview underground space that sends up everything from Brönte novels and Tennessee Williams plays (its flagship show is *Cast on a Hot Tin Roof*) to Biblical epics and Shakespearean tragedies (*As We Like It*). While there are some laughs generated from the few standout actors, the long form can end up getting, well, long.

The spoken word... Since the demise a few years ago of a legendary club called Lower Links, performers have scattered across a handful of theater spaces and clubs. They've been welcomed by the **Lunar Cabaret**, a homey Lake View restaurant and performance space that counts local songstress and performance artist Jenny Magnus among its collective owners. The venue often books local performers for extended runs. If you feel like you've stumbled into someone's home, you're right: Many of the owners are members of the offbeat musical and performance group Maestro Subgum and the Whole, who live upstairs. Performance artists do off-the-wall work at **Randolph Street Gallery**, a cutting-edge multimedia gallery (heavy on conceptual art) that brings in polished out-of-towners like the Pomo Afro Homos and the Sacred Naked Nature Girls. This River West gallery also nurtures local artists, often sandwiching intimate artist-led workshops between two back-to-back weekends of performances.

The celluloid scene... Too many of Chicago's grand old movie palaces have been demolished (the biggest of them all, the shuttered Uptown, is listed as one of 11 buildings nationwide on a preservation group's most-endangered list). That makes going out to see a first-run art film at the independently owned **Music Box Theater** a real joy. Built in 1929, the Lake View movie house has been lovingly preserved with all of its charms intact—its pink-neon marquee, the twinkling-starred ceiling on which clouds drift by, the rousing live performances by a tuxedoed organist before each weekend show.

Downtown on Michigan Avenue, the **Fine Arts Theatre** screens more mainstream foreign and independent releases for longer runs in the century-old Fine Arts

Building. The lobby retains some of its vintage character, though the theater has been carved into four nice but not extraordinary auditoriums. Hot films may run for weeks and weeks here. Serious film freaks looking for harder-to-find independent and foreign films have a few film outlets from which to choose. **Facets Multimedia**, in Lincoln Park, is the most active art-film center, presenting Chicago premieres, revivals, and American independents on video and film, and hosting several different film festivals during the year. Perhaps the biggest in the country, its video rental library has no fewer than 27,000 titles—it can cause hours of deadlock when you're looking for just the right flick. Other cinematheques include **Chicago Filmmakers**, a Wicker Park arts group that holds weekend screenings of experimental and independent fare in its Kino-Eye Cinema; and the **Film Center at the School of the Art Institute**, which selects films along monthly themes and provides academic lectures and discussions to illuminate it all. It's the place for Ingrid Bergman retrospectives and festivals of Hong Kong films (including a visit by Jackie Chan).

You really need to have been born circa 1970 or possess an acute sense of irony to enjoy the second-run fare featured at **Brew & View** at the Vic Theater in Lakeview. Gen-Xers suck down beer and eat pizza while enjoying these double features of camp, comedy, and cult faves; all movies, especially the silliest Hollywood schlock like *Speed*, elicit gleeful outbursts from the peanut gallery. It can be a real hoot.

Classical sounds... It's easy to slip into hyperbole when referring to the Chicago Symphony Orchestra, but we'll do it anyway. The 110-member body, now under the baton of musical director Daniel Barenboim, is one of the country's top orchestras, in large measure because of a peerless brass section chaired by one of the world's finest trumpeters, Adolph Herseth, and its principal hornist, Dale Clevenger. A traditionally strong wind section also makes the CSO popular among fans of Strauss, Mahler, and the later works of Beethoven. Their home base, **Orchestra Hall**, is undergoing a $100 million renovation and expansion to add additional seating and to finesse the acoustics. (People like to say that CSO founder Theodore Thomas died a few weeks after Daniel Burnham's concert hall debuted in 1905, so horrified was he by the acoustics, but don't believe them—the sound has always been pretty good.) When the renovation is completed in the fall of 1997, the complex will be renamed the Symphony Center. Along with the CSO, Orchestra Hall hosts a series of jazz, classical, and chamber music concerts, piano recitals, and the occasional pop singer. Also playing at Orchestra Hall, the Chicago Civic Orchestra, the CSO's "farm team" of students and semiprofessional musicians, has a similar repertoire, but experiments more with new works by young composers—it's easier for them to do that, since their tickets are free.

Classical sounds, summer edition... The Chicago Symphony Orchestra shares its summer home, the pastoral North Shore music venue **Ravinia Park**, with visiting orchestras, chamber music ensembles, and soloists. Though the music ostensibly draws people to this idyllic, tree-covered spot, there's also the competition to out–Martha Stewart everyone else with your outdoor-concert accoutrements: to bring the china or not to bring the china? (Do bring a citronella candle or some bug spray, though.) If you're not equipped for moonlight picnicking, you can pick up a boxed meal and also rent chairs ($3.50 each) at the well-stocked concession area. The **Grant Park Music Festival**, one of the last free classical concert series in the country, offers concerts at the Petrillo Music Shell in downtown Grant Park a couple of nights a week, as well as special evening performances by the Grant Park Symphony Orchestra and the Grant Park Symphony Chorus, composed of members of the Lyric Opera and of other vacationing musicians. Skip the grass and move up front to avoid the amplified version of events on stage. It's usually pretty easy to do: Empty seats in the season-ticket-holders section are released 15 minutes before each performance.

Chamber music... Despite its name, the **Chicago String Ensemble** is really closer to an orchestra, with 22 top-notch musicians comprising one of the few professional string orchestras in the country. For their performances at area churches, the well-respected group—which has been around since 1977—draws from an eclectic repertoire, from the classical canon to contemporary Chicago composers. Since its founder and longtime conductor resigned in the fall of 1995, it remains to be seen how this group will weather the future. The midsize orchestra **Chicago Sinfonietta** is a diverse group of musicians performing a program that's wide-ranging, to say the least. They'll perform anything from Beethoven to a contemporary jazz-inspired work accompanied by projected images of African and African-American art; guest artists might be anyone from top CSO players to Ramsey Lewis and his trio. Dusty works from the 16th, 17th, and 18th centuries are the emphasis of **Music of the Baroque**, a well-regarded chorus and orchestra drawn from the ranks of the CSO, the Lyric Opera, and others. They've made several recordings and presented the Chicago premieres of works by Mozart and Monteverdi. Various faux Gothic churches provide the architecture and the acoustics for these baroque concerts. Drawing from all different musical periods, **Chicago Chamber Musicians** has developed a reputation as one of the Midwest's finest chamber ensembles. Down in Hyde Park, the **University of Chicago**'s Chamber Music Series features visiting ensembles like the Berlin Philharmonic Quartet and the Grammy-winning Emerson String Quartet.

All that jazz... The **Chicago Jazz Ensemble**, a professional jazz orchestra in residence at Columbia College, has wowed audiences in concerts at area colleges, club dates, and outdoor festivals (both the Chicago and the Montreal jazz fests), and local clubs. It helps that the founding conductor, William Russo, is an old pro who has played over the years with Dizzy Gillespie, Stan Getz, and Duke Ellington, and was the composer and trombonist with the Stan Kenton Orchestra in the 1950s.

Night at the opera... You gotta love a woman who has the chutzpah to fire Luciano Pavarotti. A legend in the opera world herself, Lyric Opera of Chicago boss Ardis Krainik (who is set to retire in 1997) gave the heave-ho to the superstar tenor in the late eighties, after he had canceled one too many performances. She's done just fine without him, putting together a string of financially successful and artistically ambitious seasons that have vaulted the company into the ranks of the opera world's heavy hitters. Performing at the impressive **Civic Opera House**, the Lyric's works range from sturdy hall-of-famers to at least one 20th century work a year, many of which are world premieres, such as *McTeague.* While it doesn't have the high-powered glamour of the Lyric—superstar tenors, vast choruses crowding the stage, and Social Register crowds—the **Chicago Opera Theatre** makes arias accessible to a wider audience. There are some virtuoso moments, though serious opera fans will probably be disappointed. But tickets are cheaper, and easier to get, than Lyric tickets, and the company's downtown theater is intimate enough so that everybody gets to see the action (as opposed to the view from the Lyric's nosebleed upper balconies). Most of the operas are American works, as opposed to the Lyric's more traditional repertory, and are sung in English (no supertitles!).

Women in tutus, men in tights... Using a variety of venues around town for its shows and festivals, Chicago dance often gets lost in the shuffle among other performing arts—a situation that should change in another year, with the completion of the new midsize Chicago Music and Dance Theatre downtown. Classical ballet has long struggled to find a foothold in Chicago, but it now has several companies vying for support. The internationally known Joffrey Ballet fled New York in search of a more secure financial situation and landed in the Windy City in 1995 as the reconstituted **Joffrey Ballet of Chicago**. After some apprehension locally about the carpetbagging troupe, other companies have welcomed the newcomers (who still spend much of the year out of town), and audiences flocked to the group's inaugural performances. Led by a former New York City Ballet dancer, Daniel Duell, **Ballet Chicago**—which at one time considered merging with the Joffrey—has turned out to be a blip on the cultural radar, with infrequent productions and not even a permanent corps of dancers. It has been trying to rebuild, though, with an annual story ballet.

Guided by Broadway veteran Lou Conte, the globe-trotting **Hubbard Street Dance Chicago** has an exclusive arrangement to perform certain pieces by Twyla Tharp (she even created a piece for the troupe) and has earned star status with its technical mastery. Founded in 1978, the 20-member troupe is known for a high-flying, high-energy blend of jazz, ballet, and modern dance that tends to be crowd-pleasing from beginning to end. Hubbard Street dancers often make the leap from **River North Dance Company**, a younger, hipper 12-dancer troupe strong on jazz. Its brand of dance tends to be commercial, though highly skilled, MTV-inspired choreography. A focal point for modern dance in the city, the **Dance Center of Columbia College** provides a venue for some 50-plus performances a year, featuring a lot of hometown talent as well as touring guest artists from around the world. Though some shift to other venues, most are shows are at the college's intimate, no-frills 250-seat Uptown theater.

Other dance... The widely touring and ever-popular **Muntu Dance Theater of Chicago** conveys the African and African-American experience with vibrant tribal costumes, energetic drumming, and traditional dance. Not a dance group in the traditional sense by any means, **Jellyeye Drum Theatre** combines modern choreography, theatrical staging, and hyperintense pounding on custom-designed rolling drums—sort of like a thinking person's *Stomp*. Among its repertoire, *Blood Lotus* is a 40-minute nonstop tour de force of complexly choreographed rhythms.

Rock and pop concerts outdoors... **New World Music Theatre** is your basic theater-under-the-stars—it's fine when you feel like driving a million miles out to the suburbs and indulging in a rock concert spectacle with thousands of others. The view from the pavilion seats isn't all that bad, while the cheaper grass plots in back offer close-ups of teenagers making out. A mix of music, dance, and theater moves front and center at the **Skyline Stage**, a 1,500-seat open-air theater under a pristine white canopy on Navy Pier, sometimes compared (a bit generously) to the Sydney Opera House. The acoustics are sometimes spotty, depending on who's performing.

Rock and pop palaces... A few old remnants of the heyday of the 1920s in Chicago have been recycled as concert halls, including the Moorish-style **Aragon Ballroom**, an Uptown venue that for decades swung with big bands. These days the Aragon, with its atmospheric ceiling, but poor acoustics, plays host to rock performers like Alanis

Morissette; very occasionally, a Latin group or big band makes a stop here. The **New Regal Theater**, on the far South Side, is a grand old hulk of a twenties theater that looks like an Arabian fantasy, with a jewel of a mosaic-laden lobby and a (somewhat decaying) dome on top. It has been renamed in honor of another theater, now demolished, that was a renowned jazz mecca. Uptown's roomy **Riviera Theatre**, constructed in 1918 by Chicago's great theater builders Balaban & Katz, also hosts rock concerts. The suburbs have been trying to steal a piece of the entertainment pie with the new **Rosemont Theatre**.

Intimate rock halls... Before they hit stadiums (or perhaps on the long slide down), a lot of testosterone-infused rock acts come through the **Vic Theater**, a former vaudeville house in Lake View. Kids stand outside the Vic for hours, waiting to get the best seats for the occasional general-admission show. You'll practically have to shoehorn yourself into the tight cabaret seating here. Another mid-size venue, **Park West**, is a more upscale nightclub in Lincoln Park that brings in an assortment of alternative rock, reggae, and jazz acts; there's not a bad seat in the house, but, to get the best one, check to see if table reservations are taken. The balcony is a nice perch from which to take in the show. You'll find a mix of folk, country, bluegrass, and other traditional forms at concerts sponsored by the **Old Town School of Folk Music**, the oldest training ground for fiddlers, banjo players, and yodelers in the country. All the major players, from Pete Seeger to Alison Krauss, have been welcomed here. Plans are afoot for it to expand to larger quarters from its 300-seat house. An eclectic newcomer, the **Lunar Cabaret**, was established by a collective of bohemian actors and performers with a dual mission: Tired of working as waitstaff at other people's restaurants, and needing a place to perform, they set up their own cabaret space for a wild, refreshing mix of avant-garde theater and mostly acoustic music.

The Index

Annoyance Theatre. This troupe's wide-open warehouse theater in Wrigleyville presents late-night gross-out antics onstage.... *Tel 773/929–6200. 3747 N. Clark St., Red Line Addison el stop.*

Aragon Ballroom. Big bands as in big, loud, rock bands like postpunkers Green Day still play at this ex-ballroom.... *Tel 773/561–9500. 1106 W. Lawrence Ave., Red Line Lawrence el stop.*

Auditorium Theatre. Architects Adler and Sullivan's 4,300-seat masterpiece offers the finest acoustics in the city. These days it often hosts touring Broadway blockbusters. A real treat.... *Tel 312/559–2900 (Ticketmaster Arts Line). 50 E. Congress Pkwy., Red Line Jackson & State el stop.*

Bailiwick Repertory. The stage lights rarely go dark in the complex's three theater spaces, with a constant stream of provocative plays opening here....*Tel 773/883–1090. 1229 W. Belmont Ave., Red Line Belmont el stop.*

Ballet Chicago. This small classical-ballet group's precarious situation is even shakier now that the Joffrey Ballet has come to town.... *Tel 312/251–8838. Office, 185 N. Wabash Ave., suite 2300.*

Brew & View. Watching a second-run flick is a truly communal experience at this multitiered theater serving a scruffy young crowd. There's pizza and a full bar with lots of drink specials (cheap pitchers on Monday). Midnight shows on weekends.... *Tel 773/618–VIEW. The Vic Theatre, 3145 N. Sheffield Ave., Red Line Belmont el stop. Closed on concert nights.*

Cafe Voltaire. It's a crapshoot, quality wise, for the independently produced shows fermenting seven nights a week in the raw basement of this veggie restaurant. Two to three different shows run back-to-back on weekends. First come, first seated.... *Tel 773/528–3136. 3231 N. Clark St., Red Line Belmont el stop.*

Chicago Chamber Musicians. This classical group performs October–May at midsize concert halls at both Northwestern University and De Paul University.... *Tel 312/558–1404. Office, 70 W. Madison St., suite 4000.*

Chicago Filmmakers. A Wicker Park film group, which offers classes on making movies, screens documentaries, and independent and experimental works on weekends in its 200-seat theater.... *Tel 773/384–5533. 1543 W. Division St., Blue Line Division el stop. $6 nonmembers, $3 members.*

Chicago Jazz Ensemble. This 20-member repertory jazz group plays from the entire history of jazz, with particular emphasis on the works of Duke Ellington.... *Tel 773/261–9708. Office at 600 S. Michigan Ave.*

Chicago Opera Theatre. This opera company emphasizes American performers and composers and uses a midsize theater, hoping to make opera inviting to a non–black-tie crowd. The season runs June–July.... *Tel 773/292–7578. Merle Reskin Theatre, 60 E. Balbo Ave., Red Line Harrison/State el stop.*

Chicago Sinfonietta. This racially diverse 45-member orchestra performs six programs a year, September–May, at downtown Orchestra Hall, suburban River Forest, and one free concert at the South Shore Cultural Center on the South Side.... *Tel 312/857–1062. Office, 105 W. Adams St.*

Chicago String Ensemble. The city's only professional string orchestra gives four concerts a year, September–May, often showcasing world-class soloists and introducing rising young stars.... *Tel 312/332–0567. Office, 3524 W. Belmont Ave.*

Chicago Theatre. This 4,000-seat theater at the head of State Street has been restored as a performing arts center, used for visiting musicals and occasional concerts.... *Tel 312/ 902–1500 (Ticketmaster). 175 N. State St., Red Line Washington & State el stop.*

Civic Opera House. A-list singers, spectacular sets, and this regal house make the Lyric Opera of Chicago one of the toughest-to-find tickets in town. The season runs September–February.... *Tel 312/332–2244. 20 N. Wacker Dr., Brown Line Randolph and Wells el stop.*

Court Theatre. Affiliated with the University of Chicago, this theater embraces classic French literature, Shakespeare, and other highbrow stuff in its September–May season.... *Tel 773/753–4472. 5535 S. Ellis Ave., Metra train to 57th and Lake Park Dr. stop.*

Dance Center of Columbia College. This hub for modern dance in the city has performances September through May, with both a resident company and guest artists.... *Tel 773/989–3310. 4730 N. Sheridan Rd., Red Line Lawrence el stop.*

ETA Creative Arts Foundation. A highly regarded African-American company stages serious drama in its 200-seat theater, including several productions geared for families. On Mondays, look for staged readings of new plays in its workshop.... *Tel 773/752–3955. 7558 S. Chicago Ave., Metra train to 75th St. stop.*

Facets Multimedia. At this nonprofit film center's small theater, you may feel like you've got your own private screening room, albeit one with uncomfortable seats.... *Tel 773/281–4114. 1517 W. Fullerton Ave., Red Line Fullerton el stop.*

Film Center at the School of the Art Institute of Chicago. A curated cinema program screens four to five movies a week in a congenial auditorium.... *Tel 312/443–3733. Columbus Dr. and Jackson Blvd., Red Line Jackson & State el stop.*

Fine Arts Theatre. Downtown, this chain-owned quartet of auditoriums shows commercial "art" films.... *Tel 312/ 939–3700. 418 S. Michigan Ave., Red Line Jackson & State el stop.*

The Free Associates. Practitioners of long-form improvisational comedy, the troupe uses audience input to concoct one-act plays based on a sharp ear for literary genres.... *Tel 773/975–7171. Ivanhoe Theater, 750 W. Wellington St., Red Line Belmont el stop.*

Goodman Theatre. Despite its long-standing solid reputation, Goodman doesn't seem afraid to take a few risks, even on its main stage, a comfy 700-seat theater with pleasing sight lines and a proscenium-arch stage.... *Tel 312/443–3800. 200 S. Columbus Dr. (east side of the Art Institute), Red Line Monroe & State el stop.*

Grant Park Music Festival. The Chicago Park District's summer concert festival presents a raft of free performances June–August by the Grant Park Symphony Orchestra and soloists occasionally as illustrious as Van Cliburn.... *Tel 312/819–0614. Petrillo Music Shell, Grant Park, Columbus and Jackson drives, Red Line Jackson & State el stop.*

Hubbard Street Dance Chicago. The city's premiere homegrown dance troupe will be based at the Chicago Music and Dance Theatre when it opens in 1998; until then, the ensemble performs in April and May at various sites around town.... *Tel 312/663–0853. Office: 218 S. Wabash Ave.*

ImprovOlympic. Co-owned by a former Second City director, this club brings together Chicago's top improvisers for Monday jams, as well as more structured shows staged upstairs in a 100-seat space. In the downstairs cabaret theater, workshop students give unscripted performances.... *Tel 773/880–0199. 3541 N. Clark St., Red Line Addison el stop.*

Jellyeye Drum Theatre. This powerful performance group shouts and bangs on drums with abandon.... *Tel 773/278–6371. Office, 1513 N. Western Ave.*

Joffrey Ballet of Chicago. Led by cofounder and artistic director Gerald Arpino, this 30-dancer classical ballet troupe incorporates members of the former New York company and a few dancers scooped up from Ballet Chicago (see above).... *Tel 312/739–0120. Office, 70 E. Lake St., suite 1300.*

Latino Chicago Theater Company. Presenting original productions by Latino writers, the theater is located in an ex-firehouse in the gentrifying Wicker Park/Bucktown are.... *Tel 773/486–5120. 1625 N. Damen Ave., Blue Line Damen el stop.*

Lookingglass Theatre Company. The theatrical adaptations and original plays from this young company can get a bit ponderous, but are always filled with beautiful images. They perform at a variety of venues.... *Tel 773/477–9257. Office, 3309 N. Seminary Ave.*

Lunar Cabaret. The restaurant's menu is mostly veggie, while the theater, performance art and music (jazz, folk, klezmer), presented in a cabaret setting, are gathered from the fringes.... *Tel 773/327–6666. 2827 N. Lincoln Ave., Brown Line Diversey el stop. Closed Mon.*

Mercury Theater. This new 300-seat playhouse was designed as a venue for fresh off-Loop theater and performance art.... *Tel 773/325–1700. 3745 N. Southport Ave., Brown Line Southport el stop.*

Metro. A Chicago institution, this sturdy old theater packs in throngs of alternative-rock fans. Save on Ticketmaster fees by buying advance tickets at the club's box office. Shows sell out quickly.... *Tel 773/549–0203. 3730 N. Clark St., Red Line Addison el stop.*

Mexican Fine Arts Center Museum. Located on the Lower West Side, in the Mexican neighborhood of Pilsen, this museum has nurtured several local fledgling Latino theatrical groups.... *Tel 312/738–1503. 1852 W. 19th St., Blue Line 18th St. el stop.*

Muntu Dance Theatre of Chicago. The popular African ethnic dance company draws upon traditional and contemporary dance styles.... *Tel 773/602–1135. Office, 6800 S. Wentworth Ave.*

Music Box Theater. This elegant, beloved theater in Lake View presents an eclectic bunch of independent and subtitled foreign films, hosts both the Chicago International Film Festival and the Chicago Lesbian and Gay International Film Festival, and runs midnight shows too.... *Tel 773/871–6604. 3733 N. Southport Ave., Brown Line Southport el stop.*

Music of the Baroque. A series of eight annual concerts are given by this established chorus and orchestra, October–May.... *Tel 312/551–1414. Office at 100 N. LaSalle Dr., Suite 1610.*

Neo-Futurists. Located above a funeral home, this theater group offers one-acts and other experimental stuff. They don't take reservations, so show up early for their long-running hit *Too Much Light Makes the Baby Go Blind.... Tel 773/275–5255. 5153 N. Ashland Ave., Brown Line Montrose el stop, transfer to 9 Ashland bus.*

New Regal Theater. This vintage South Side venue is dark a lot of nights, but occasionally brings in big-name singers or performing acts.... *Tel 773/721–9230. 1645 E. 79th St., Red Line 79th St. el stop, transfer to #79 bus.*

New World Music Theatre. Big-ticket rockers take the stage at this suburban open-air stage. Well, at least you're outside.... *Tel 312/559–1212 (Ticketmaster). 19100 S. Ridgeland Ave., Tinley Park. No el stop nearby.*

Old Town School of Folk Music. This long-established school presents not only folk acts at its 300-seat concert hall and other venues in the city, but also jazz, world music, Native American, Celtic, Latin, and Cajun. A Sunday showcase series introduces emerging artists.... *Tel 773/525–7793. 909 W. Armitage Ave., Armitage el stop.*

Orchestra Hall. This sublime 1905 hall, designed by Chicago's great architect and planner Daniel Burnham, is home to the Chicago Symphony Orchestra, the Chicago Civic Orchestra, and visiting jazz, classical, and chamber artists.... *Tel 312/435–6666. 220 W. Michigan Ave., Jackson el stop.*

Park West. This intimate, cabaret-style music club has a way of focusing attention on the stage.... *Tel 773/929–5959. 322 W. Armitage Ave., 151 bus from North Michigan Ave. or State St.*

Randolph Street Gallery. This River West gallery is also a performance art mainstay for locals and name artists coming through town. Shows often sell out in the black-box theater.... *Tel 312/666–7737. 756 N. Milwaukee Ave., Blue Line Chicago el stop.*

Ravinia Festival. A romantic spot to relax on the lawn and hear music on a summer evening. The festival runs June–September; the rest of the year, recitals featuring musicians under age 30 are held in the park's Bennett Hall ($15).... *Tel 312/RAVINIA (728–4642). Lake-Cook and Green Bay roads, Highland Park; Metra train to Ravinia Park stop.*

River North Dance Company. Performing at various venues October–May, this 12-member jazz-oriented company gives local artists a shot at choreographing.... *Tel 312/944–2888. Office: 1016 N. Dearborn Pkwy.*

Riviera Theatre. "The Riv" is an ex–movie palace in Uptown, turned rock and pop concert venue.... *Tel 773/275–6800. 4746 N. Broadway, Red Line Lawrence el stop.*

Roadworks Productions. Another fresh band of eager thespians making a go of it in the crowded Chicago theater world.... *Tel 773/489–ROAD. Office: 1532 N. Milwaukee Ave.*

Rosemont Theatre. This new suburban venue for pop concerts and Broadway shows has little charm, but the sound and sight lines in the theater are terrific.... *Tel 847/671–5100 info; tel 312/902–1500 Ticketmaster phone orders. 5400 N. River Rd., Rosemont.*

Royal George Theatre Center. A Lincoln Park theater complex usually engaged with long-running mass-appeal musicals or dramatic fare.... *Tel 312/988–9000. 1641 N. Halsted St., Red Line North & Clybourn el stop.*

The Second City. An Old Town institution—launching pad for comedic careers from Ed Asner to Gilda Radner to the voice of Homer Simpson (Dan Castellaneta)—with a wall of glossies to prove it. There's no drink minimum, so all ages are welcome in the main-stage space and the adjunct Second City e.t.c.... *Tel 312/337–3992. 1616 N. Wells St., Brown Line Sedgwick el stop.*

Shakespeare Repertory. The Bard is all that this ten-year-old company does, and they do him well. The audience surrounds the stage on three sides of the 333-seat theater. Season runs October–May.... *Tel 312/642–2273. Ruth Page Theater, 1016 N. Dearborn Pkwy., Red Line Clark & Division el stop.*

Shubert Theatre. Beware the second balcony and a few obstructed seats in this otherwise magnificent 2,000-seat theater, the home of a subscription series of touring Broadway shows.... *Tel 312/902–1500. 22 W. Monroe St., Red Line Monroe el stop.*

Skyline Stage at Navy Pier. An open-air theater is part of the reinvigorated Navy Pier entertainment complex.... *Tel 312/595–7437. Grand Ave. at Lake Michigan, Red Line Grand el stop, transfer to 65 Grand or 29 State buses.*

Steppenwolf Theatre Company. This widely admired, risk-taking company still seems to be growing into its big, boxy theater complex, which includes a 500-seat main stage and an upstairs studio space.... *Tel 312/335–1650. 1650 N. Halsted St., Red Line North and Clybourn el stop.*

Theatre Building. More than a dozen theater companies, including some promising young upstarts, use the three spaces in this Lake View complex.... *Tel 773/327–5252. 1225 W. Belmont Ave., Red Line Belmont el stop.*

Theatre on the Lake. Tickets are cheap and the productions pretty good at this Lincoln Park theater. The season runs June to August; order seats by credit card over the phone or in person at the box office.... *Tel 312/742–7994. Fullerton Ave. and Lake Shore Dr., 151 Sheridan bus.*

Torso Theater. This shabby Lake View storefront theater pushes the boundaries of taste, with campy material appealing to a late-night Gen X audience.... *Tel 773/549–3330. 2827 N. Broadway, Red Line Belmont el stop.*

University of Chicago Chamber Music Series. In the university's fine concert hall, some celebrated visiting ensembles make their Chicago appearances.... *Tel 773/702–8068. Mandel Hall, 57th St. and University Ave., Metra train to 57th St. and Lake Park Dr.*

Vic Theater. Dating to the teens, this small Lake View theater doubles as a rock venue and second-run movie house (see **Brew & View**).... *Tel 773/472–0366. 3145 N. Sheffield Ave., Red Line Belmont el stop.*

Victory Gardens Theater. This Lincoln Park company stages five main-stage plays a year by contemporary writers, while three other theaters are rented out to young go-get-'em troupes.... *Tel 773/871–3000. 2257 N. Lincoln Ave., Red Line Fullerton el stop.*

spo

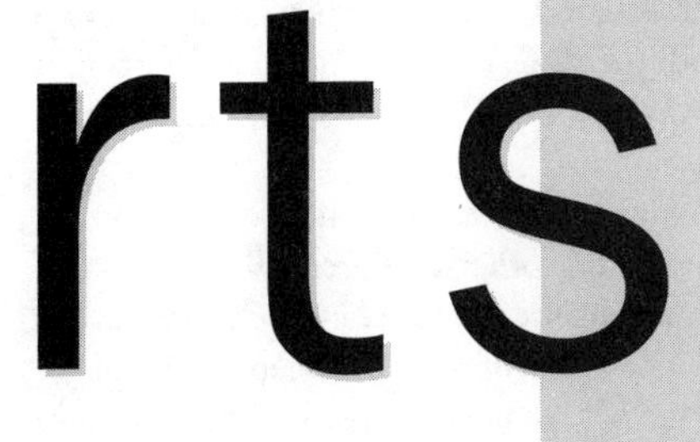

“Saturday Night Live” sealed the image of Chicago as a city of Superfans: rib-gnawing, beer-guzzling simpletons convinced that their teams can do no wrong. Of course, come to think of it, SNL wasn't too far off the mark. Just try making your way through one of the brats-and-Old-Style tailgate parties in Soldier Field's parking lot before a Bears game.

Professional sports are taken very seriously here, and it's just assumed that everyone keeps up with them. Even if you're not Da Most Sports-minded guy or gal, you may feel a bit silly getting all gussied up for a club only to learn that everybody else in town is huddled around a TV worshipping the Bulls. As true sports diehards, Chicagoans know that winning isn't everything. With teams like the Cubs in town, finding new ways to toss off phrases like "there's always next year" has evolved into a high art. But Chicagoans are a loyal bunch and embrace all their teams, good and bad—they've found room in their hearts for both the Bulls *and* the Cubs. For sports fans it's all the same, anyway. You don't love or hate a team so much as obsessively fixate on it.

While football fans embrace the brutal cold they call "Bear weather," Chicagoans otherwise aren't the most outdoorsy folk. And can you blame them? They've adapted to the climate with a range of indoor options for keeping the blood going. The city has one of the most extensive park systems in the country, with plenty of free facilities (open until 10pm) where visitors can work out. There's also no shortage of private health clubs and fitness centers that welcome out-of-towners with a (paid) guest pass; your hotel may have negotiated special rates with a nearby club, so be sure to inquire. Come spring, the sight of joggers, bladers, and bicyclists along the lakefront well past twilight is enough to stir the most recalcitrant athlete.

The Lowdown

Where to watch

Hoop dreams... There are really only two words that need to be said about the **Chicago Bulls**. Repeat after me: Michael Jordan, Michael Jordan, Michael Jordan. The citizens of this fair city became positively suicidal in 1993 when he retired to chase fly balls, went practically orgasmic when he un-retired two years later, and were simply awestruck by the sublime season His Airness made possible in his first full year back—a new NBA record, with 72 regular-season wins and a fourth championship. As if that didn't provide enough excitement, Dennis Rodman has done the impossible, eclipsing Jordan's celebrity with his mischief on and off the court. A Rodman mural for a local men's haberdashery literally stopped traffic on the Kennedy Expressway. What was the fuss? Rings, tattoos, and an Armani jacket sans sleeves (strong stuff for the Midwest). Tickets to games at the sparkling new **United Center** (tel 312/455–4000; 1901 W. Madison St., 20 Madison Bus), the successor to the famously earsplitting Chicago Stadium, are some of the toughest in town—the cheap seats cost only $15 (if you can get them), but a courtside spot goes for $325.

Peanuts and Cracker Jack... Going out to a baseball game in Chicago requires a little soul-searching. You've got to choose sides. American League or National League? North Side or South Side? Blue collar or blue blood? While the Sox and Cubs will compete in 1997 for the first time (under a newfangled bastardization of baseball rules), there's always been a deep-rooted rivalry between the cross-town teams. White Sox fans tend to be hardcore baseball lovers, drawn from the bungalows of the

South Side and south suburbs, who often deride the North Side's **Chicago Cubs** as a yuppie team. Cubs fans like to pretend that the South Side doesn't exist, so it ends up a wash. **Wrigley Field** (tel 773/404–2827; 1060 W. Addison St., Red Line Addison el stop), home of the Cubs and one of baseball's oldest, most esteemed parks, occupies a special place in everyone's hearts, not only in Chicago but all over the country thanks to cable-transmitted WGN-TV. The lovable losers haven't made it to the World Series since 1945 (even then they lost the Series) and have gone to the playoffs just three times since Harry Truman sat in the Oval Office. Yet the bleachers are filled every game, day or night (tickets run $9 to $19), with fans drawn by the park's ivy-covered outfield, quaint manually operated scoreboard, and the legendary announcer Harry Caray.

Wrigley Field survived the addition of lights in 1988, though some neighbors fought bitterly to oppose the change. The team now plays fewer than 20 night games at home, but purists still duck work to bake in the bleachers for afternoon games. The surrounding streets (Sheffield and Clark) are populated with all kinds of ethnic restaurants and sports bars that take on a carnival atmosphere on game days. During night games, parking is restricted to residents with zoned permits; so don't risk it; your car will be gone when you return from the game. Try one of the lots ($10 or more), or, better yet, let the el drop you off at the park's front door.

While Cubs fans show up just for the experience of the "Friendly Confines," **White Sox** fans arrive at the new **Comiskey Park** (tel 312/924–1000 for team offices, 312/831–1769 for Ticketmaster; 333 W. 35th St., Red Line Sox/35th el stop) to watch the game. Or so they would have you believe. The city's South Side team has played consistently better than the Cubs over the years—the Sox even made it to the American League championship in 1993—but the fans can be fickle. They've been saddled with a soulless new mallpark and even Saturday night fireworks can't compete with the devotion Chicagoans hold for the other ball club. They've also been saddled with possibly the most unlikable owner in baseball, Jerry Reinsdorf, who threatened to take the team to Florida if the city didn't ante up for the "Sterile Confines" of the new Comiskey. The Sox play about a quarter of their schedule under lights at Sox Park; tickets are $8 to $18.

Pigskin... While baseball divides the city, football brings it together: The **Chicago Bears** (tel 847/615–2327; Soldier Field, Lake Shore Drive and 16th Street, Red Line Roosevelt el stop) still enjoy the good will brought by NFL founder and former owner George Halas Sr.; his son, coach George "Papa Bear" Halas Jr.; and a tradition of big-name players from Dick Butkus to William "Refrigerator" Perry. It's been a few years since he led the team, but Mike Ditka, the prototype for the SNL gag, still retains the moniker "Da Coach." But the Bears have been testing fans' patience by kvetching about their need for a fancy new dome and skyboxes to replace Soldier Field; they've threatened to move out of the city—even across the border to Indiana (!!!)—if they don't get their way. All this talk prompted Mayor Daley to say that he didn't care if the team moved to Alaska. While most games are held on Sunday afternoons, a couple are regularly scheduled for Monday evenings. Season tickets passed down through the generations have contributed to years of sold-out games at Soldier Field. If you miss the early summer offering of single tickets ($33, for end-zone seats only), your best bet is going through a ticket broker, showing up at the game hoping to find a few (scalped) extras, or packing a parka for a frigid late-season game when saner fans stay home by the TV.

Slapshots... The defense-oriented **Chicago Blackhawks** (tel 312/559–1212 for Ticketmaster; United Center, 1901 W. Madison St.; 20 Madison bus) have made the National Hockey League playoffs several times in recent years, but a poor draft over the last decade has kept the team in the league's second tier. Still, don't think of showing up to root for the other team. Just about everybody—hardworking people, from factory workers to CEOs—shows up at the United Center draped in the team's red hockey jerseys, and they can barely contain their cultish fervor throughout the playing of the national anthem. Their impassioned vocalizing made the old Chicago Stadium death-defyingly loud, which really threw visiting teams off their game; the larger United Center has diluted things a bit, but you should still observe three rules at a Blackhawks game: 1) Hate the longtime owners, the Wirtz family, and never, never forgive them for trading away Bobby Hull more than two decades ago; 2) When the players set up for a power play, shout "SHOOT! SHOOT!" at the top of your lungs; and 3) No matter how much the team sucks, stick by the hardworking players, knowing that you love hockey and no one else in town really cares. Tickets cost from $15 to $75 and are easy to get for most games.

Where to play

Bowled over... Chicago is a bowler's kinda town. One of the real gems is **Southport Lanes & Billiards** (tel 773/472–6600; 3325 N. Southport Ave., Brown Line Southport el stop), a former Schlitz tavern in Lake View that's been lovingly preserved by its new twentysomething owners. No computerized scoring here: Bowling pins are even reset by youthful human pinsetters, the same way they were when the four vintage lanes were installed here in the 1930s (a sign helpfully warns: "Remember, if you see legs—don't bowl."). The yuppie neighborhood crowd also enjoys the nice billiards room, bar area, and sidewalk patio. You won't find many bowlers donning "Jimmy D's Trucking" team shirts at **The Lucky Strike** (tel 773/549–2695; 2747 N. Lincoln Ave., Brown Line Diversey el stop), a slick Lincoln Park bar/restaurant that has elevated the working-class sport to high art. Eight automated Brunswick lanes were rescued from a since-demolished bowling alley and packaged with a traffic-stopping movie-style marquee, 1920s Deco fixtures, and vintage French advertising posters. Expect pretty decent food, a nice poolroom, and boutique beers on tap (brands no doubt served for the first time in a bowling alley).

The exuberant neon sign outside and orange-accented lanes inside—so numerous they seem to fade into the horizon—give a glamour of its own to **Marzano's Miami Bowl** (tel 773/585–8787; 5023 S. Archer Ave., Orange Line Pulaski el stop) on the Southwest Side. *This* is a bowling alley: 80 lanes, open 24 hours, cheese popcorn from the vending machine, corn dogs at the grill, and regular Joes and Janes of all races and ages wearing T-shirts with slogans like "Shut Up and Bowl." A perfect score.

Pool on cue... The pool sharks at **Chris's Billiards** (tel 773/ 286–4714; 4637 N. Milwaukee Ave., Blue Line Jefferson Park el stop) are so serious that music is an unnecessary distraction. One soundproof chamber has a token jukebox. The main room is eerily silent: All you hear is the solid clack of billiard balls. Devotees of all ages and races bring their own pool cues in little black cases to this second-story mecca near O'Hare Airport. With 41 tables, Chris's, which was used as a location for filming *The Color of Money* and has the framed photos and newspaper clippings to prove it, sponsors weekly nine-ball tournaments, brings in pros for big-money competitions, and runs a complete pro shop. Games are a bargain at $7 an hour, and the place is open until 1am nightly. **The Corner Pocket** (tel 773/281–0050; 2610 N. Halsted St., Red Line Fullerton el stop) is a wood-paneled Lincoln Park neighborhood hangout that didn't fall victim to the yuppie pool hall trend of a few years back: The nine handsome regulation-size tables are slick enough, yet the place is populated by young locals of the baseball-cap-wearing variety yapping about the Cubs. You've got to be a little wary of any place that hypes itself on a Top 40 radio station—with that in mind, venture to the River North club **Lucky's** (tel 312/751–7777; 213 W. Institute Place, Brown Line Chicago el stop), a loft space trying to be hip, with big velvet curtains, Jazz Age murals, faded Oriental rugs, and a dozen tightly packed tables. The crowd of office-partyers, big-haired and big-muscled suburbanites, and 9-to-5ers on their way home seem more interested in mixing and mingling than they do in shooting and sinking. There's a dress code (no gym shoes or torn jeans) and a cover charge after 9pm for men. You won't find a singles scene at **St. Paul Billiards** (tel 773/472–9494; 1415 W. Fullerton Ave., Red Line Fullerton el stop), a relic of a pool hall up in Lincoln Park, where a dozen tables are lit by bare fluorescent bulbs in a decrepit room. There's a jukebox and a snack bar where the owner, whose grandfather opened the place, greets customers, but there's no bar, which may account for the small turnout—it's never hard to get a table here.

For gym rats... Winter-weary Chicagoans spend so much of the year waddling about under bulky sweaters and Michelin Man-esque parkas that health clubs beckon like human hothouses. What may be the country's poshest health club, the downtown **East Bank Club** (tel 312/527–5800; 500 N. Kingsbury St., Brown Line Merchandise Mart el stop) is a half-a-million-square-foot colossus—you can imagine archaeologists unearthing it someday far, far in the future and preserving it as a lost city of a fitness-crazed civilization. The club where Oprah does her predawn crunches spoils its Who's Who members with amenities up the wazoo: entire cavalries of stationary bikes and climbing machines, four swimming pools, an indoor driving range, a pair of running tracks, a restaurant, a hair salon, complimentary everything in the locker room, and even private nap rooms where you can catch a few winks between sets of reps. All that said, the club, open until 11pm, doesn't offer daily guest passes; to get in, you're going to have to either befriend a member or belong to the same network of upscale health clubs. The McDonald's of health clubs, **Bally Total Fitness**, operates an outpost in the Loop (tel 312/372–7755; 25 E. Washington St., Red Line Washington/State el stop) that's convenient for downtown workers and, as a result, is predictably overcrowded. Open until 9pm weeknights, the club is equipped with the usual weight and cardio machines, swimming pool, steam room and sauna, and aerobics studio. Like a pair of gray sweats in a spandexed era, **Webster Fitness Club** (tel 773/248–2006; 957 W. Webster Ave., Red Line Fullerton el stop) is refreshingly unpretentious: At this corner gym in Lincoln Park, the weight machines are ancient, the sound system is a boom box, and there are only a half a dozen stairmonsters and a couple of treadmills. It's open until 9:30pm weeknights, and you can get in for $10 a visit.

The latest aerobics fads often show up first at **Jamnastics Fitness Center** (tel 773/477–8400; 2727 N. Lincoln Ave., Brown Line Diversey el stop), a Lincoln Park complex with a nice weight room and a weekly offering of nearly 60 aerobics classes ($8 to $10 per class) with heart-racing titles like street jam and cardio jazz. It's open weeknights until 9:30pm. You'll have time to contemplate how much your body aches from aerobics classes at the softly lit space at **Zen Fitness** (tel 312/280–9166; 22 E. Elm St., Red Line Clark/Division el stop). This Gold Coast studio gives working out a New Age spin by dedicating the last few minutes of every class—from cardio pump to power yoga—to relaxation and meditation, and offering sessions in tai chi, yoga, and breathing. It's open most nights until 8:30pm; a class will set you back $13.

Fun runs... The lakefront is the obvious destination for anyone with the inclination to run, but visitors should use common sense when running after dark. While the path through **Lincoln Park** is pretty well lit, there are a few dark, isolated stretches and the asphalt has some rough patches that might be difficult to see. The lighted, quarter-mile track in **Lake Shore Park**, at Chicago Avenue and Lake Shore Drive, is a safer alternative, a quick jog away for visitors staying in hotels on North Michigan Avenue.

Several organized running groups welcome visitors on their early evening runs. Most follow the lakefront for five miles or so and often go en masse for dinner at a local restaurant. Check with the **Chicago Area Runners Association** (tel 312/922–4420) for a complete list of clubs, schedules, and running tips. On the north side, **Lincoln Park Pacers** (tel 773/477–8818) meet Tuesdays at 6:30pm at the runners' bulletin board in the park, at Diversey Parkway and Cannon Drive; **Frontrunners/Frontwalkers** (tel 312/409–2790), a lesbian and gay running group, meet at the same time and day farther north, at the totem pole at Addison Street and Lake Shore Drive; and the **Chicago Women's Running Club** (tel 773/743–0061) has a weekly Wednesday outing that begins at 6pm at Foster and Lake Shore Drive. On the south side of the city, the **Rainbow Road Racers** (tel 773/324–5524) convene at 6:30pm Wednesdays at the Point (55th Street and Lake Shore Drive).

For something completely different, tag along with the **Chicago Hash House Harriers** (tel 312/409–2337), a good-humored group whose slogan is "a drinking club with a running problem." Starting and ending at a tavern, the weekly "hashes" are unpredictable 3- to 5-mile courses identified only with chalk marks or scraps of toilet paper. The group's Tuesday runs (and monthly full-moon dashes) have led unsuspecting participants down Lower Wacker Drive, through back alleys, and across streams in forest preserves. Call for the week's starting point.

In the swim... In the summer, you'll find plenty of fearless kids jumping into Lake Michigan's languid surf, but the water is so damn cold until the dog days of August that for most Chicagoans "swimming" in the lake means daintily dipping their toes and running back to the beach. Serious swimmers, many of them triathletes in wet suits, flock to the chest-deep water along two separate ledges running from Ohio Street to North Avenue, where they can swim half a mile uninterrupted in a straight line. In the summer, the Chicago Triathlon Club puts buoys in the water off Ohio Street Beach at the quarter- and half-mile mark and has members on hand twice a week in the early evening. The lake is watched over by lifeguards from late May to Labor Day and is open for swimming until 9:30pm.

When it's too chilly or choppy outside, try one of the two dozen city pools that offer free lap-swimming in the evening; call the park district (tel 312/747–0829) for locations and hours. The **Chicago Smelts** (tel 312/409–4974), a "mostly" gay and lesbian masters team, welcomes all amphibious-oriented types to coached workouts that are held four nights a week at the city pool at Gill Park (tel 773/742–7802; 833 W. Sheridan Rd., Red Line Sheridan el stop). For the cost of a guest pass, **Lakeshore Athletic Club** (tel 312/477–9888) in Lincoln Park has several workouts a week of varying competitive levels.

While many of the downtown hotels advertise what amount to little more than glorified bathtubs, the Mag Mile's **Hotel Inter-Continental Chicago** (tel 312/944–4100; 505 N. Michigan Ave., Red Line Grand el stop) has the real thing high atop its thirteenth floor: an elegant, Italianate, junior Olympic-size (25-meter) natatorium adorned with stained glass and mosaic tiles. You might expect to see Esther Williams come bubbling up to the surface any minute, and in fact these waters were once churned by Olympic legend and *Tarzan* star Johnny Weissmuller. Nonguests can use the pool (and adjoining health club) for $13 a session until 9pm.

The tennis racket... Chicagoans try to spend every possible opportunity playing outside when the weather warms up, so the park district's lighted tennis courts along the lakefront are indeed popular on summer evenings. You can't just breeze onto a court; most require either reservations or waiting your turn. There are a dozen courts in Grant Park at **Daley Bicentennial Plaza** (tel 312/742–7648 for general info, 742-7650 for reservations; 337 E. Randolph St., Red Line Randolph el stop) that rent for $5 an hour and stay open until 10pm. Reservations are accepted the day before; the courts go fast, so be ready with the speed-dial first thing in the morning. Farther north, courts at **Waveland** (tel 312/742–7674, Addison Street and Lake Shore Drive, Red Line Addison el stop or 151 Sheridan Bus) require a $3 daily fee and accept in-person reservations only. Both sets of courts are open from April to October. You may have better luck finding court time farther inland at the park district's **McFetridge Sports Center** (tel 773/478–0210; 3843 N. California Ave., Brown Line Irving Park el stop, transfer to 80 Irving Park bus), which has both outdoor and indoor courts open pretty late (call for schedules). Rates are $13 to $15 plus a $3 registration fee, and reservations are taken up to six days in advance.

You can hardly find a decent place to eat past 10pm in Chicago, but you can play tennis until midnight on the 18 indoor courts operated by the biggest private tennis center in town, **Mid-Town Tennis Club** (tel 773/235–2300; 2020 W. Fullerton Ave., 74 Fullerton bus). Only USTA members or other affiliated club members can use the tennis center (which also charges for court time), but if you manage to glom onto a member, the $12 guest fee is waived on Friday and Saturday nights. The downtown **Lakeshore Athletic Club** (tel 312/644–4880; 441 N. Wabash Ave., Red Line Grand el stop) sponsors social mixers on the weekend, for folks who want to burn off calories with a game of doubles and then put them back on with an after-set round of beer and pizza. A daily guest pass to the club is $15.

Skate away: wheeler-dealers... Yes, times *have* changed. Rollerskates have nearly gone the way of the dodo bird, and the biggest rink in Chicago frisks its customers, checking for weapons. But **Rainbo Roller Skating Center** (tel 773/271–6200; 4836 N. Clark St., 22 Clark bus) is still a fun late-night party spot. A disco nap helps: The largely African-American contingent of skaters, who check out each other's moves on and off the floor, don't show up before midnight, and they stick around until 4am to skate-dance under the huge mirrored skyline and constellation of glimmering disco balls, to a mix of soul, pop, and R&B tunes. The rink also has special family, children's, and teen skates. You can rent or bring your own skates; rentals are $2.25 for skates, $3.50 for in-lines. Admission is $5 to $8.

There's no better place to Rollerblade skate outdoors in warmer months than along the lakefront, either heading south to Adler Planetarium or north to Oak Street (where freestylers show off) and up to Diversey. During twilight the busy scene can resemble a Third World highway free-for-all, with skaters, cyclists, joggers, and errant toddlers vying for a stretch of the asphalt path. Consider seeking safety in numbers by joining the conga line of bladers that blasts off weekly from **Londo Mondo Motionwear** (tel 312/751–2794; 1100 N. Dearborn St., Red Line Clark/Division el stop), a Gold Coast skate and apparel shop. The throng of skaters, whose numbers swell to 100, snakes through downtown and the Near North Side and caps the hour-long skate with drinks at a local bar. Show up with skates on Wednesdays at 6:30pm from April to September.

Skate away: icing it... Chances are, if you do any skating in Chicago, it'll probably be on ice. For the past few winters, Chicagoans have skated in the heart of downtown at **Skate on State** (tel 312/744–3315; State St. between Washington and Randolph Sts., Red Line Washington/State el stop), a large rink that sits like a canyon surrounded by Marshall Field's flagship department store, City Hall and various office towers, and Karl Wirsum's whimsical *Plug Bug* mural. If the whole operation looks a bit temporary—this isn't the ice at Rockefeller Center by any means—that's because it is. The whole block was razed in the late 1980s for a massive office complex that never materialized, and lately developers have been sniffing around again with a few ideas for the block. (In the summer, the space is converted into Gallery 37, a city-sponsored student art program.) The rink, which has a warming hut and concession stand, is open until 7:30pm from November to March. Skating is free if you have your own blades, $2 to $3 if you need to rent.

There are a couple of other nighttime skating options in the winter, including the outdoor rink at **Daley Bicentennial Plaza** in Grant Park (tel 312/742–7650; 337 E. Randolph St., Red Line Randolph el stop) and an ice-cube-sized surface at **Navy Pier** (tel 312/595–PIER; 600

E. Grand Ave., Red Line Grand/State el stop), which gets a bit frosty on Chicago's brisk February nights—thank gawd there's a warming shed offering hot chocolate here.

Fore!... Even after the sun sets on the eighteenth hole, golfers hoping to prep for tomorrow's game can still squeeze in a few practice swings at several lighted driving ranges in Chicago. And you can get from the Loop to the links in mere minutes. Located blocks from Michigan Avenue, **Illinois Center Golf** (tel 312/616–1234; 221 N. Columbus Dr., Brown Line State/Lake el stop) is the kind of thing you might see in Japan. When the real estate market bottomed out a few years ago, developers went with the unusual concept of building a lush nine-holer, the first urban golf course in the country. With the remarkable sight of the skyline as a backdrop, golfers can choose from nearly 100 hitting stations, a dozen of which are covered and heated in the winter; balls cost from $6 to $14 per bag. The par-three course is open year-round and stays open until 9pm in summer, with a $19 fee; it may get lights for nighttime play in 1997.

The Chicago Park District has a couple of lighted driving ranges with 40-plus hitting stations, open at night from April to October. On the North Side, there's a driving range (and 18-hole miniature-golf course) at **Diversey** (tel 312/747–7929; Diversey Pkwy. and Lake Shore Dr.) with half of its stations heated and covered; on the South Side, there's an unheated range in **Jackson Park** (tel 312/747–2762; Lake Shore Dr. and 63rd St.). Buckets of balls cost from $4 to $6.

Having a (paint) ball... A curious thing happens even to people who think only geeks play paintball: Once they strap on a color-coded team vest, get armed with an air rifle loaded with gelatin-filled "bullets," and disappear into the **Chicago Paintball Factory** (tel 312/563–1777; 1001 W. Van Buren St., Blue Line UIC Halsted el stop), the most timid pacifists are soon sniping about the 35,000-square-foot River West warehouse like raging Rambos. For $18 an hour you too can play combat in this postapocalyptic maze of junked VW Bugs and neon graffiti; the paintball center is open until 10pm nightly, with reservations required 24 hours in advance for both teams and individuals. Go ahead, make your day.

hangi

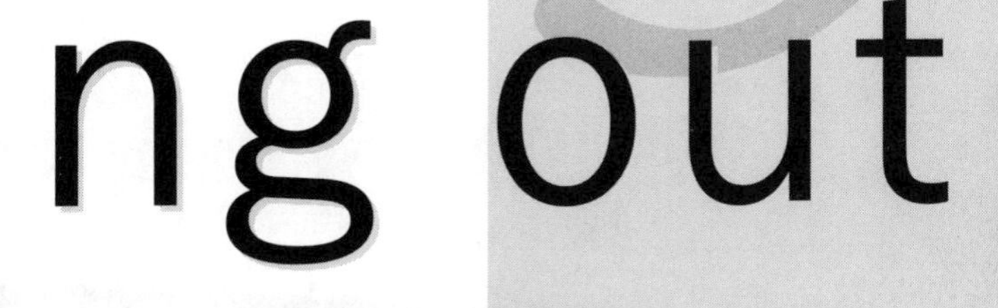

"Make no little plans," declared the great Chicago architect and planner Daniel H. Burnham. Of course, he was referring to city building, while you may be interested in something more along the lines of a laid-back Friday night, when picking a direction to walk or settling into a good bookstore is your greatest ambition. But in a way, Burnham's visionary Plan of Chicago paved the way for your Chicago *un*-plan: His 1909 blueprint for the city makes it possible for today's visitors to reach the lake's edge at the rejuvenated Navy Pier, stroll across the Chicago River and up past the enticing shop windows of North Michigan Avenue, or plunk down to marvel at the city's architectural showpieces from a landscaped vantage point in Grant Park. Thanks to Burnham, there are plenty of things to do in Chicago without doing much.

The Lowdown

Best views (free)... There's no better place to feel the power, history, and romance of Chicago than with your feet firmly planted on the **Michigan Avenue Bridge**. One of 20 movable downtown bridges that span the river, this bridge and its four ornamented pylons opened in 1920 are lit like a movie set, flags waving in the wind on each side. Turn 360 degrees and take in the monuments to the building boom of the 1920s, standing like giants on the river's edge: on one side, the gleaming terra-cotta Wrigley Building, bathed in 116,000 watts of light beamed from the river's south bank, and the Gothic-style Tribune Tower; on the other side of the river, the old Stone Container Building and the Art Moderne tower of 333 North Michigan. Fittingly, this is where Chicago began: the city's first permanent resident, Jean Baptiste Point du Sable, set up his cabin on the river's north side. Where the river meets Lake Michigan, **Centennial Fountain** (McClurg Court and the north bank of the Chicago River) sends a continuous arc of water streaming 80 feet high and 200 feet across the river like a kind of urban geyser. Visible from the Michigan Avenue Bridge it faithfully fires up for 10 minutes every hour on the hour, until midnight, from May to October. But there are few water shows that compare to **Buckingham Fountain** (at Congress Pkwy. and Columbus Ave. in Grant Park)—you know, the one shown in the opening credits of "Married... With Children." The three-tiered Beaux Arts fountain, built in 1927, is even grander than its inspiration, the Latona Fountain in Versailles, and was rehabilitated in 1995 to great nighttime effect: its shifting colored light-show glows brighter, the dancing waters of its bronze sea horses and marble basins are more vigorous, and its main plume blasts higher than ever, 165 feet into the sky.

You really have to step way back to get a good look at the vastness of the city. The north side of **Adler Planetarium** (1300 S. Lake Shore Dr.) obliges with a sweeping view of the entire skyline from across Monroe Harbor. You almost feel like you're sitting on an island watching the city. In warm weather, the romance of the setting after dark inspires couples to lounge on the grassy slope or dangle their toes at the water's edge, listening to the distant sound of sirens and watching circling airplanes zip over the city like fireflies.

Make someone else drive when you're cruising down **Lake Shore Drive**, which offers one of the best overviews of the city, day or night. Heading south from North Avenue, the skyline of North Michigan Avenue appears: The **John Hancock Center**, the tallest structure in view, tapers to its top, where a band of bright white light girdles the building. In recent years, Chicagoans have looked to the skyscraper for some small-town-style seasonal cheer: red and green at Christmas, orange at Halloween, purple when Northwestern University made the 1996 Rose Bowl, and red as the Bulls sailed on to their fourth title. Lake Shore Drive winds around primo highrise homes at Oak Street Beach and south past the flashing lights of the **Navy Pier's Ferris wheel**; the drive ascends the bridge at the Chicago River, where the shimmering commercial towers unfolding to the west look like little toy models, and then pours into Grant Park.

Best views (for a fee)... Chicago has a great pair of skyscraping perches for peering out over the city at night. Which one you choose depends upon what you're looking for. The **Sears Tower** has the obvious marquee value, though Chicagoans are still a bit shell-shocked to find that they've been second city-ed again—and not by New York or L.A., but by twin towers in Kuala Lumpur, Malaysia, which have officially replaced architect Louis Sullivan's modernist monolith as the world's tallest building. But Sears Tower's marketing folks have resisted redoing all those brochures and elevator announcements, and they do have a point: Visitors to the 103rd floor **Sears Tower Skydeck** (tel 312/875–9696; 233 S. Wacker Dr., enter on Jackson Blvd.), could thumb their noses down on folks in the highest *occupied* floors of the spire-topped 88-floor Malaysian skyscrapers. The Skydeck's open until 10pm, October through February, and even later, until 11pm, March through September; admission is $4 to $6.50. While the view from the Sears Tower is impressive, especially the western view of the city's street grid outlined by streetlights, the observatory of the elegant X-braced **John Hancock Center** (tel 312/751–3681; 875 N. Michigan Ave.) offers a more diverse panoramic view, and it's open as late as midnight. From the 94th floor, you can follow the lake's shoreline and Lake Shore Drive north, and the entire Loop (including the Sears Tower) to the south. For your money, you get an even better value two flights up in the building's **Signature Lounge**: A drink will run you about the same as a $5.75 observatory ticket.

One of the newest attractions on the cityscape is the **Ferris wheel at Navy Pier** (600 E. Grand Ave., 312/595–PIER), a reproduction of the original that debuted at the 1893 World's Colombian Exposition (a k a the world's fair). Flickering with white lights in positively psychedelic patterns, the 15-story wheel offers a seven-and-a-half-minute ride that's slow enough for riders to memorize the skyline, and it costs a measly $3. It only operates May through October, but the big wheel keeps on turning as late as 10pm Sunday to Thursday and midnight Friday and Saturday.

The city takes on an entirely different look from the lake, a sight that, shamefully enough, more tourists than locals have probably enjoyed. A growing fleet of **boat cruises** departs from both Navy Pier and the Chicago River for one- to two-hour sunset and night excursions year-round that package dinner, drinks, and dancing for $25 to $80. Many coast by the shoreline and make special stops for the Buckingham Fountain light show. Boats docked on the south side of Navy Pier run the gamut from supersleek ones like ***Odyssey II*** (tel 708/990–0800), a 700-passenger yacht that makes summer moonlight cruises of the lake after midnight ($27 per person), to the four-masted schooner ***Windy*** (tel 312/595–5555; $15–20) to the 70-foot speedboat ***Seadog*** (tel 312/822-7200; $11–16). And the Gray Line of boating, **Wendella Sightseeing Boats** (tel 312/337–1446, northwest corner of lower Michigan Avenue at the Chicago River), gives three narrated tours of the lake and river each night, from April through October, for prices ranging from $5.50 to $11.

Clattering and squeaking down the tracks, the **el** (tel 312/836–7000) offers a big-city thrill of its own and a truly Chicago experience. There's nothing glamorous about it—it's grungy and jostling—but for a buck and a half it gives a pretty good tour. Try to grab the front seat on a train's lead car for a real amusement-park–ride experience. The Brown Line (still called the Ravenswood by locals) provides the best views, starting at ground level on the nearly pastoral North Side, then rising above the rooftops past North Avenue to offer glittering views of downtown's western profile. Next it crosses the Chicago River and heads into the Loop—the elevated tracks that encircle the downtown core give it that moniker.

Best walks... Well suited for after-dinner perambulations, **North Michigan Avenue** is brightly lit and busy with racing cabs, packs of business travelers and other out-of-towners, and the occasional Rollerblader zooming down the sidewalk. A heart-healthy walk would start at the north end of the street, at Chicago Avenue by the brightly illuminated historic Water Tower (a limestone pumping station that survived the Chicago Fire of 1871), then progress south past Neiman Marcus, NikeTown, and all the rest until you reach the river. The street is especially festive during the December holidays, when thousands of twinkly white lights are strung from the trees, from the river up to **Oak Street**, which is well worth a nighttime stroll on its own account. This quaint street with antique streetlights is lined with a row of blockbuster European designer boutiques, from Armani to Versace. (Save your window-shopping for nighttime, when the shops here are closed, and save a bundle.) Crossing Oak is **Rush Street**, where you'll join the flow of revelers hopping to restaurants and nightclubs. Rush Street long ago shed its go-go party image of the seventies and eighties, but there are still some good spots in the neighborhood that keep it thriving after dark, especially in warm weather when some of the clubs operate bustling sidewalk cafes or throw open their doors to the street.

People huddle at night around **Buckingham Fountain** in Grant Park as though it were a giant liquid bonfire; the perimeter is populated with families, little kids wearing those glow-in-the-dark necklaces, and snuggling couples absorbing the fountain's light show, which ignites nightly at 9pm from May to October and cycles toward a midnight finale. A nice stroll would begin at the ceremonial gateway to Grant Park at Michigan Avenue and Congress Parkway. Each side of Congress Plaza, which was recently restored, is flanked by larger-than-life equestrian Indian statues, the Spearman and the Bowman. Head east up the steps and into the park. You can't miss the fountain. For a long walk on a not-so-short pier, trek over to 3,100-foot-long **Navy Pier**, which was originally built in 1916 and has been transformed into a convention and entertainment spot with restaurants, tchotchke shops, and theaters. While the redesign is a bit bland, the pier nonetheless has become a hopping waterfront night spot (especially in warm weather) with concerts, fireworks, a beer garden, and jugglers, clowns, and musicians entertaining crowds of tourists and suburbanites. In addition to its signature Ferris wheel, the Pier also keeps the kiddos busy whirling around on a carousel of 38 handpainted animals; rides are $2.

Best alternatives to a taxi... **Horse-drawn carriages** have become a fixture in Chicago, much to the chagrin of impatient motorists and one uptight city alderman who tried a few years ago to put diapers on the beasts. Until 2am on weekends, half a dozen different companies pick up passengers looking for a nostalgia trip from carriage stands near the intersection of Michigan and Chicago avenues. Decked out in Victorian garb, the drivers will take you past whatever scenery you prefer, from the gleaming malls of North Michigan Avenue to the old-money brownstones of the Gold Coast. Many of the carriages are antique or Amish-made, and are ready for any weather: The tops come down in the summer, while wool blankets are provided for snuggling in snowy months. Companies will also provide champagne, roses, and drivers who only speak when spoken to. Rides are generally about $30 per half hour, and reservations are not necessary, though they're a wise idea during the Christmas holidays (and, of course, prom season). The city's oldest and largest carriage operator is **Noble Horse** (tel 312/266–7878).

For a taste of Bangkok right here in Chicago (and we're not talking noodles), hitch a ride in the back of a **pedicab**. During warm weather, about half a dozen freelance drivers congregate at various key locations with their brightly colored, three-wheel vehicles (the "love-children of the bicycle and the rickshaw," as one driver calls them): You'll find them around Wrigley Field on game nights, at Rush Street or the Halsted/Lincoln bar corridor, and at summer festivals and concerts. For about $5 a half mile, these easygoing pedal-pushers will ferry you back to your car or on a short tour of the neighborhood. You may feel a little silly riding in the open-air seat, but before long you'll be waving to folks on the sidewalk like a Rose Bowl Parade queen.

Late-night shopping... Most of the merchants on North Michigan Avenue, the city's premier shopping district, ease customers out the door by 7pm. You can squeeze in a further hour at **Marshall Field's** (tel 312/335–7800; 835 N. Michigan Ave.) at Water Tower Place, **Bloomingdale's** (tel 312/440–4460; 900 N. Michigan Ave.), and **FAO Schwarz** (tel 312/587–5000; 840 N. Michigan Ave.), while Water Tower's **Lord & Taylor** store (tel 312/787–7400; 835 N. Michigan Ave.) tops them all with a 9pm last call.

On nearby Rush Street attached to the big Starbucks, the yuppie record store **Hear Music** (tel 312/951–0242, 932 N. Rush St., Red Line Chicago/State el stop) gives all of its folk, blues, jazz, and alt.rock CDs the sheen of a J. Crew catalogue where sage-colored T-shirts seem better than green. This store groups records by categories like "perfect dinner music," "backyard bar-b-que," and "the dark side of love." You also get to thumb through the fave artists of your favorite artists in bins holding top choices by people like John Cale, Roseanne Cash, and Dave Brubeck. It stays open until midnight on Friday and Saturday and 10pm during the week (11pm in summer).

Shops are open until 9pm weeknights and 10pm weekends (and even later in summer) at two waterside attractions, **North Pier Festival Marketplace** (tel 312/836–4300; 435 E. Illinois St., Red Line Grand/State el stop, transfer to 29 State St. bus) and **Navy Pier** (tel 312/595–PIER or 800/595–7437; 600 E. Grand Ave.), but tourists are the only people you'll find here. North Pier, a smartly rehabbed shipping warehouse on an extension of the Chicago River, has a more eclectic mix of 40 shops, several restaurants with dockside terraces, and a sprawling third-floor kids' paradise of video games, minigolf, and virtual reality diversions. Located within walking distance, directly east, Navy Pier harbors more typical impulse-buy fare, with about a dozen stores aimed mostly at kids, including a children's book and toy store, a shop with souvenirs from Chicago museums, and an outlet of the hometown independent Barbara's Bookstore. In the summer, about 50 retail and food vendors set up carts outdoors on the pier's south side along Dock Street.

After the dinner hour, most of the retail world in Chicago is the domain of Gen-X types, which translates into plenty of shops in hip neighborhoods where you can idle away the hours without ever opening your wallet. In Lincoln Park, **Tower Records and Books** (tel 773/477–5994; 2301 N. Clark St., Red Line Fullerton el stop) is an exercise in overstimulation. Open until midnight, the sprawling store offers hours of free entertainment, whether you're thumbing through the zillions of magazines, out-of-town newspapers, and 'zines, browsing the book section, listening to preselected recordings on headphones, or just checking out the with-it crowd.

Before committing to a buy, picky audiophiles can test-listen to everything—new and used, alternative and import, space age and ska—on portable CD players at **Evil Clown** (tel 773/472–3418; N. Halsted St., Red Line Addison el stop), a small Lake View store that stays open until 10pm weeknights, 9pm on Saturdays. Also offering free trial listening is **The Quaker Goes Deaf** (tel 773/252–9334; 1937 W. North Ave., Blue Line Damen el stop), a hip Wicker Park shop owned by an ex-DJ. It has a high tin ceiling, funky lamps, and stays open until midnight (Sun until 8pm). The selection is broader (even vinyl), and there's a big wall plastered with theater posters, concert flyers, and "drummer wanted" ads—basically lots of ideas for filling up the night. Both record shops even have trendy magazines to peruse while you've previewing tunes.

"Halter tops, you know, they're back in," is the kind of eavesdropped insight you pick up from the disheveled urchins rifling through thrift-store threads at **Ragstock** (tel 773/868–9263; 812 W. Belmont Ave., Red Line Belmont el stop), also in Lake View, which stays open until 10pm Friday, 9pm other nights. The big second-story shop (enter through the alley on Dayton) is crammed with both new and used clothes that have been screened somewhat; they're a notch choicer than the things you'd find at Goodwill. Main street seems to have caught up with **The Alley** (tel 773/525–3180; 858 W. Belmont Ave., Red Line Belmont el stop, open until midnight Friday, 1am Saturday), once the home-away-from-home in Lake View for any self-respecting angst-ridden teen in white pancake makeup and ratted-out black hair. You can still enter through, yes, the alley, and the place has tried to keep the faith, with murals of hell-hounds and latex mannequins ghoulishly simulating electrocutions like Disney World automatons. But now it's been bloated into an "alternative shopping complex" of several boutiques under one roof hawking leather jackets, incense, T-shirts, latex lingerie, and plaster gargoyles, becoming annoyingly commercial. Or perhaps we've just gotten old and cranky. Check out the new Wicker Park location at the intersection of North, Damen, and Milwaukee avenues (tel 773/862–5055). There's something surprisingly wholesome about squeaky clean straight couples, curious single people, and neighborhood gays shopping at **Cupid's Treasures** (tel 773/348–3884; 3519 N. Halsted St., Red Line Addison el stop), a Lake View purveyor of G-strings, adult films, flavored whip cream, and other sensual pleasures, that's open until midnight nightly (till 1am on Friday and Saturday). Try not to blush in the boutique's room devoted exclusively to dildos.

Browsing for books... Chicago has become a battleground for megabookstores—who knows which ones will survive to stock this book. At press time, **Borders Books and Music** (tel 312/573–0565; 830 N. Michigan Ave., Red Line Chicago/State el stop) was last seen rolling over the competition on North Michigan Avenue with a four-story mall of books and records that's outfitted with lots of comfy arm chairs and the de rigueur cafe. You can even browse through books at your table while gazing toward the landmark Water Tower and the rest of the Mag Mile. One advantage to sitting inside is that you don't have to look at Borders' own garish, sign-drenched exterior. In Lincoln Park, **Barnes & Noble Bookstore** (tel 773/871–9004; 659 W. Diversey Pkwy., Brown Line Diversey el stop), an airy single-story shop with the feel of a library, has been challenged a block away by another Borders (tel 773/935–3909; Clark and Diversey, Red Line Belmont el stop). All of these monsters are open until at least 11pm most nights.

With Godzilla and Mothra slugging it out around them, independently owned booksellers certainly would appreciate your business. A few good ones are **Barbara's Bookstore**'s roomy Old Town flagship store (tel 312/642–5044; 1350 N. Wells St., Brown Line Sedgwick el stop), which stays open most nights until 10pm, and **Unabridged Books** (tel 773/883–9119; 3251 N. Broadway, Red Line Belmont el stop, open to 10pm), a Lake View shop that boasts strong travel and gay sections, hosts author readings in the evenings, and employs a knowledgeable staff who flag their recent faves with insightful handwritten minireviews. We don't suggest risking the el at night to make a special trip, but if you're down in Hyde Park after dark, there's the used-book institution **Powell's Book Store** (tel 773/955–7780; 1501 E. 57th St., open until 11pm), which also has a couple of other North Side locations as well. And if you're not too sleepy-eyed to read past midnight, head over to Wicker Park's **Myopic Books** (tel 773/862–4882; 1726 W. Division St., Blue Line Division el stop), a boho used-book store with a faithful neighborhood following that the owner pushes out the door at 1am (except Sunday when they close earlier). The neatly organized shop, located on the hood's gritty slacker strip, has a basement overflowing with more books, along with random chairs and tables for sitting around drinking java.

Browsing for adult books... Of course, there are a few more "bookstores" open even later, the kind that charge a $1 browsing fee. Open around the clock, the Gold Coast location of **Frenchy's** (tel 312/337–9190; 872 N. State St., Red Line Chicago and State el stop) makes it a convenient drop-in spot for the Rush Street habitué. Besides a few aisles of skin mags, there are video rental and a small stock of porno paraphernalia and latex stuff, as well as a few dingy booths with plastic chairs for watching films as long as your quarters last. Located on a rather deserted stretch of road west of downtown and near the United Center, **Erotic Warehouse** (tel 312/226–5222; 1246 W. Randolph St., Green Line Ashland el stop), also open 24 hours, is one of the more spacious and cheerily lit shops of its ilk, with a copious assortment of magazines, videos, R. Crumb comics, blowup dolls, and wicked novelty items. You can browse glossies or pay a $10 cover to gain entrance to a maze of rooms in the back for more "hands-on" shopping at **The Ram** (tel 773/525–9528; 3511 N. Halsted St., Red Line Addison el stop), a gay bookstore open until 6am in the heart of Boys Town.

Museums after dark... There's something luxurious about being able to linger over Monet wheat stacks or make eye contact with eels while Chicago's world-class museums run up their electricity bills for a few hours after dark. Better yet, these once-a-week late evenings often feature free admission, too. On Tuesdays, there's no charge at the city's treasured **Art Institute of Chicago** (tel 312/443–3600; 111 S. Michigan Ave., Orange Line Adams el stop) when it stays open until 8pm and the crowds are visibly thinner than on packed weekends. A monthly After Hours soirée here offers an even better opportunity to view the museum's endless galleries in near total privacy, because the attending hordes of young professionals with noticeably naked ring fingers are too busy queuing up for the cash bars and posing on the Grand Staircase. The few who actually make it into the galleries do so only after a few drinks, when everything begins to look like an Impressionist masterpiece. These events are free for museum members, $5 for their guests and $10 for everybody else. Wednesday evenings are free at the **Museum of Contemporary Art** (tel 312/280–2660; 220 E. Chicago Ave., Red Line Chicago el stop), which has made a bid for the big league with a rather austere aluminum-clad new building and outdoor sculpture garden that debuted in 1996 on a prominent site off Michigan Avenue. Five times bigger than its cramped predecessor, the museum for the first time has room to display its burgeoning permanent collection of pop, conceptual, and minimalist art, as well as examples of the city's homegrown Imagist school and a new theater for video, performance art, and other programs. The galleries stay open until 9pm on Wednesdays, and the first Friday evening of each month features a happy-hour event ($5 members, $10 nonmembers) with guided exhibition tours and special activities like performance art, music, and video art. On those same Friday evenings, galleries in the nearby **River North Gallery District** (tel 312/649–0064; Red Line Chicago el stop), the art-rich warehouse area bounded roughly by Michigan, Orleans, Erie, and Chicago avenues, keep their doors open late as well. Openings are also typically held on Fridays throughout the year, and there's a big formal seasonal kickoff in early September when all of them coordinate their openings. The city's third major art institution, the **Terra Museum of American Art** (tel 312/664–3939; 666 N. Michigan Ave., Red Line Chicago/State el stop), keeps the light on until 8pm on free Tuesdays. Terra displays a fine collection of 19th- and 20th-century works by such artists as Edward Hopper, Mary Cassatt, and John Singer Sargent.

Families especially should appreciate a slew of other museums with extended hours. The new **Chicago Children's Museum** (tel 312/527–1000; 700 E. Grand Ave., Blue Line Washington el stop), a dynamite three-level playpen where everything is hands-on, becomes a total madhouse on the free Thursday family nights; the place is crawling with wee ones whose voices reach a deafening crescendo. Or for a zoo of another kind visit the **Shedd Aquarium** (tel 312/939–2438; 1200 S. Lake Shore Dr., Red Line 12th/Roosevelt el stop), the country's largest indoor fish tank. In summer, the aquarium plays up its dramatic lakefront real estate every Thursday with a jazz band and cocktails on its north terrace, while the rest of the place stays open until 9pm. Here's a fun Friday night date: The **Adler Planetarium** (tel 312/922–7827; 1300 S. Lake Shore Dr., Brown Line Van Buren el stop) puts on one of its sky shows every Friday at 8pm (admission $4). A bit of a hidden gem is the basement-level **Bicycle Museum of America** (tel 312/222–0500; 435 E. Illinois St.,) on the east side of the North Pier entertainment complex. The Windy City location is appropriate: Back in the 19th century the city was home to Schwinn and other bike manufacturers, and Lake Street was known as Bicycle Alley. The museum's collection of two-wheelers spans their development from the early boneshakers of the mid-1800s to today's nifty mountain bikes. It stays open until 8pm Saturday evenings; admission is $2 for adults, $3 for kids.

late nigh

6

t dining

Not all that long ago, a night out on the town here meant a deep-dish pizza at Uno or Gino's East, or maybe steaks and chops "dis tick" at Lawry's The Prime Rib. Those places and their coronary-inducing brethren still exist—a quick look around at some of the beef-fed, belt-straining guts around you should prove that—but Chicago has finally matured. In a culinary sense, at least. Gone are the days when the defunct Cafe Bohemia and its zebra steaks was the most exotic dinner in town. Chefs (and bartenders, for that matter) have moved beyond the borders of the city's ethnic specialties and meat-packing past to embrace and embellish current trends in food. Authentic Mexican is hot now, a fact to which the success of Chapulín can attest, as are tapas as served at Cafe Iberico and Bossa Nova. Harry's Velvet Room serves five kinds of carpaccio and Wishbone's specialty is hoppin' John (black-eyed peas over rice with cheddar, scallions, and tomatoes).

How To Dress

Better to wear a jacket if you even think there's an iota of a chance you'll be required to don one, but frankly, unless you're scaling the heights of dining here, you probably won't have to. Chicago isn't a stuffy town, but it's no resort, either; wearing shorts and sunglasses is frowned upon at stylishly chic places like Brasserie Jo. If in doubt, dress up—you can get away with your Donna Karan tux anywhere if you're dining late after a formal event; the folks at SuperDawg will be most pleasantly surprised.

Getting the Right Table

You don't need to worry about greasing the palms of Chicago maître d's—it's not the custom here. And as far as the "right" table goes, the only one to avoid is the one near the bathroom or the kitchen. Of course, certain restaurants have truly prime tables; you can request that seating when you call for reservations, though there's no guarantee you'll get it. At most restaurants that accept reservations, you should try to call at least three days in advance. If you can, leave a phone number where you can be called to confirm (if they can't reach you, they may drop your reservation).

The Lowdown

All night long (after midnight)... When the host at **Cafe Iberico** says the wait for a table is "20 minutes," it can translate into 5 or 50, depending. Still, it's open late, it's in trendy River North, it's cheap, and it's just the kind of food—tapas—you want at the end of the evening. You'd better stop at a cash machine before eating at the **Ritz-Carlton Cafe** because, face it, osso bucco at midnight in the cafe of one of the toniest hotels in town doesn't come cheap. For those whose activities lead them to *need* late night munchies (and you know who you are), hit **Johnny Rocket's** for their great chili dogs, **The Wiener Circle** for fabulous hand-cut fries, or **The Melrose** for thick French toast. If you're down at the University of Chicago, **Medici** is one of the few late-night spots and, lucky for you, serves really good pizza (what would you expect, considering half of their customers are college students?). At **Bar Louie**, the noise, if nothing else, will keep you up, though the pizzas and sandwiches will definitely please. A few blocks away, there's **Harry's Velvet Room**, a decadently swanky joint that's dark enough to let you get away with not looking too hot by the end of a long night. It attracts a weird congregation of beautiful people, club kids, bikers, and too-rich-for-their-own-good traders. Another bastion of cool, **Iggy's** serves late and attracts a biker and biker-wannabe crowd. Chinese food has a way of satisfying those late-night hunger pangs like no other cuisine, and though most of Chinatown goes pretty dead late at night, two places—**Hong Min** and **Tin-Yen**—serve top-notch Cantonese food until the wee hours. Lastly, when a craving for Korean cuisine comes over you (or just a desire for something *really* different), try the **Korean Restaurant**, open 24 hours a day.

Before or after the show (downtown)... There isn't a huge choice of restaurants downtown—the Loop gets pretty quiet after the brokers and their secretaries take off for home—but if you're going to the Shubert or Goodman theaters, the **Italian Village** is a reasonably priced old stalwart. It's been around since 1927 and remains a fancy-schmancy kind of place for City Hall types. Not far away is **Russian Tea Time**, which serves hearty Russian fare. Be warned, though; blinis, borscht, and the like may have you nodding off long before poor Judd is dead.

Before or after the show (on the North Side)... Don't even think about getting a pretheater table at **Trattoria Gianni** without a reservation. It's a stone's throw from both Steppenwolf and the Royal George Theater and it's packed every show night right up till curtain, at which point it empties out. Up the block a bit, and less tied to the tides of the theatergoing public, is **Chapulín**, an upscale restaurant specializing in regional Mexican fare. Both **Cullen's Bar & Grill** and **Strega Nona** sandwich the Mercury Theater, as well as the arty-film-showing Music Box; good burgers and beer at sports bar–like Cullen's; unusual pastas at Strega Nona, in a lively atmosphere. **Ann Sather** is near a lot of the small hole-in-the-wall theaters in Lake View and serves the sort of eggs-and-sandwiches type food that doesn't distract from an argument about the performance-art piece you just saw. Also nearby is **Dish**, which serves vaguely Mexican food (lots of salsa as a side dish) and killer margaritas.

Après-clubbing... At **The Wiener Circle** in Lincoln Park, the short-order cooks behind the counter may scream at you, but it's generally well-meaning: "WHAT DO YOU WANT? FRIES WITH THAT? COME ON, COME ON, FRIES?" The answer should always be yes, no matter what they ask. Everything on that? Yes. Extra salt? Yes, Yes, Yes. These guys are hot dog and hamburger professionals, and if they can't satisfy your late-night hunger, nobody can. After a night at the bars (mostly gay bars) on Halsted and Broadway in Lake View, the people-watching continues at **The Melrose**, a popular diner serving around the clock. **Bar Louie** for Italian sandwiches and beer, and **Cafe Iberico** for a panoply of tapas. All are near to the River North nightclub scene, and each, in its own way, delivers a soothing culinary end to an evening.

People, people who watch people... Of course, it depends on whom you want to see and by whom you want to be seen. For instance, though some say it's yesterday's restaurant, head to **Bice**, where dinner is fed to Chicago's version of Euro-trash. Besides swarms of folks from its Lake View neighborhood, **Mia Francesca** attracts such a modelly crowd that half the time everyone's heads are spinning around like a room full of possessed Linda Blairs. But it's not only the crowd that's hot, so is the food—designer pizzas and pastas that never miss. There is also a lot of neck-craning at **Gibsons Bar and Steakhouse**, a swinging steak house on Rush Street, but not typical of Rush Street; it's filled with middle-aged divorcées, cigar-chomping guys wearing huge pinkie rings, sleek trophy-wife wannabes, visiting celebs, and neighborhood rich people in search of strong drinks from a heavy-handed bartender and steaks the size of Rhode Island. No one said it was *better* than typical Rush Street places; just different. It takes a bit of effort to get to and into the French-inspired bistro **Marché**, which is always crowded yet doesn't take reservations for prime dining hours; but the payoff is a crowd so eye-blindingly fab that it's almost as good as a night at the theater. At **Club Lucky**, a takeoff of a 1940s supper club, you can catch up-and-coming artists and their dressed-in-black friends discussing the latest Karen Finley act or the new show at that tiny basement gallery up the block. It's a total power scene at **Brasserie Jo**, where the city's elite meet to eat and be seen and talk and be seen and drink and be seen. Chef Joho's usually walking around greeting his pals, which makes you wonder who's out back cooking up the coq au vin. If a little al fresco people-watching is your style, catch the crowds from the sidewalk cafes at **Tempo** or **The Third Coast**, each of which will let you sit for hours drinking cup after cup of coffee.

Beauty's in the eye of the beholder... Though there are easier restaurants to get to than **Marché**, this grand bistro, located in the up-and-coming River West neighborhood, is well worth the cab fare for the oh-so-chic atmosphere. Wrought metal and lush swathes of velvet fabric make the room look like a large version of the killer's in *Silence of the Lambs*. Don't let the porn shop next door keep you away from **Brasserie Jo**, a French beauty in River North with mural-covered walls and an authentic zinc-topped bar. **Ben Pao**'s dramatic black interior makes this new, upscale Chinese restaurant, also in River North, seem as if you're eating moo shoo pork inside a black lacquer box. It's hard to believe that **Hacienda Tecalitlan** was built only a year ago—its lovely open-air, 19th-century-inspired courtyard seems a century old.

Deals on meals, part one (under $10)... At **Nueva Leon** in Pilsen you get authentic Mexican roadside food at dirt cheap prices. In Bucktown, the pan-Asian noodle dishes and satays at **Hi Ricky** (short for hello, Richard?) all come in for only a few bucks but satisfy at a much higher rate. And at the **Billy Goat Tavern** you not only get cheap burgers, you get abused by a short-order cook straight out of a "Saturday Night Live" sketch.

Deals on meals, part two (under $25)... The most gorgeous people in town continue to eat at **Mia Francesca**, not only because gorgeous people like to stick together, but because of moderate prices and consistently good trattoria food. At **Yoshi's Cafe** you get a lot of choices for your money, just not much bang for your buck. The pizzas are tiny, the salads are tiny, and even the marinated tofu steak is tiny. That said, though tiny in size, it's all big in flavor. There's no wishy-washiness about **Wishbone**, a sprawling Southern-style place in an out-of-the-way location west of the Loop; half the joint is a regular restaurant with waiter service, the other half a cafeteria (at lunch, at least; there's table service at dinner), but both sell hearty country food at country prices. Grungy **Leo's Lunchroom** wears its lack of pretentiousness like a badge of honor (have a pierced nose and you'll fit right in), but, despite the shabby atmosphere, the food's terrific and inventive, with some really creative fish and chicken dishes. In fact, Leo's spawned a nearby competitor, the equally grungy **Twilight**, with its downscale look and upscale menu. Crowds indicate that the word is out, about **Club Lucky**, where the wait can go on forever. It looks a little like a forties diner, with plenty of Naugahyde banquettes and an uninspired Italian menu, but the atmosphere and the Wicker Park location are definitely "now." The sprawling space has good sight lines that make it possible to see who's cutting deals with whom, who's sending drinks to whom, and who's basically doing whom. None of the stir-frys or Asian noodle dishes at **Big Bowl** cost more than $10, but after you add in an order of Thai spring rolls and one of their unique ginger drinks, you're probably spending twice that.

Hot dog stands... And what do the regular guys eat after they've had their fill of Old Style at the corner tap? Rest assured they are not ordering carpaccio, nor are they puzzling over a list of tapas. They are eating hot dogs, slopping Italian beef juice on their Bulls T-shirts, and grabbing handfuls of big, greasy fries. And they are having fun. Italian beef is a sandwich made of thin-cut beef stewed in its own juices, seasoned with Italian spices in a length of Italian bread. Order it wet, for full effect. Sweet peppers are up to you. By the way, hot dogs here don't get slathered with kraut or other mystery condiments; Chicago takes pride in its colorful and identifiable wiener adornments like fresh tomatoes, relish, onions and such. The following are tried-and-true homes of native on-the-go cuisine: Near De Paul University there's **Demon Dogs**, and far to the northwest there's **SuperDawg**. You'll know you're at the latter by the large barbell-toting hot dog on the roof. **Gold Coast Dogs** on State Street is worth a try and **Portillo's**, though infected with an "Old Chicago" theme-park ambience, is a better bet for authentic food than its national chain neighbors like Hard Rock Cafe. And like the name says, there are great wieners with all the fixin's at **The Wiener Circle**.

Pizza... Despite all you've heard about Chicago-style pizza, no one eats that stuffed pizza all the time. Are people in China eating General Tso's Chicken a couple times a week? No, those massive, three-inch-thick pies are for special occasions. Chicagoans like to eat, but they don't have a death wish. Your everyday, average Chicago pizza is still a bit different from what you'll find elsewhere, though. Sausage in clumps, toppings under the cheese, and it's all cut into little squares. Try **Pizzeria Uno**, **Giordano's**, or **Gino's East** for deep-dish. Order extra tomatoes and cheese—it's amazingly good. The wait at all of the these pizzerias is long, but you can generally order way before you're seated, so the food will be delivered not long after you hit the table. (That way they can get you in and out as fast as possible.) Parvenus—at least compared to Uno and Gino's—**Leona's** and **Ranalli's off Rush** also serve very good pizzas, and the latter has a huge list of imported beers to wash it down with. You can go almost anywhere for the usual thin-crust, but many say that **Home Run Inn** on the Southwest Side has the best in town.

Ethnic eating... It was only a matter of time when the idea of ethnic food would cease meaning only Asian and Mexican. For instance, there's **Russian Tea Time**, where the food is straight out of the Borscht Belt (badda bing, badda boom). Take some limpa bread, lingonberry sauce, and meat balls and whaddya get? **Ann Sather**, of course, a Swedish restaurant where, much to the chagrin of its patrons, the waiters and waitresses aren't all six-foot-three blond-haired gods and goddesses. In fact, far from it. Cheap is the operative word, garlicky the operative flavor at **Cafe Iberico**, an authentic, smoky, raucous River North tapas bar. All that said, however, there's lots of great Chinese and Mexican food in Chicago, including **Hong Min** and **Tin-Yen** in Chinatown. Not as good as either of these two, but much prettier (actually, anything would be prettier), is upscale **Ben Pao** in River North. For a more exotic type of Asian cuisine, try the **Korean Restaurant** in the ethnic Albany Park neighborhood. **Hi Ricky** is one of the newest and best of the pan-Asian (i.e., Japanese, Chinese, Vietnamese, Thai) noodle shops that have sprouted all over town in recent years. If only the actual countries could get along as well. Three Mexican restaurants really stand out, as well: **Nueva Leon**, a Mexican diner in the South Side Mexican neighborhood of Pilsen; **Chapulín**, a yuppie place which serves its margaritas in martini glasses; and **Hacienda Tecalitlan**, the liveliest of the bunch, with a roving 10-man mariachi.

Al fresco... At **The Heartland Cafe**, a mellow health-food-y place stuck in a 1960s time warp, the front patio tables overlook a sleepy tree-shaded side street in Rogers Park. Competition for seats outdoors at **The Third Coast** is totally cutthroat, given that most people who do get a streetside seat linger a long time. It's no wonder, though, considering this inexpensive cafe's hot location a block off Michigan Avenue. It's a real Chicago experience—really—to sit in the garden of **The Pepper Lounge**, beneath the twinkling Christmas lights they hang in summer, and listen to the el rumble by only a few feet away. For a quieter time, try the lovely outdoor garden area at **Oo-La-La!** in Lake View or at **Bice**, where a smart Gold

Coast crowd congregates to sip bellinis and grappa until all hours. Diners **Tempo** and **The Melrose** both have large outdoor seating areas and it's a good thing too, since at least the passing parade will distract you from the fact that the food is causing angina. It figures that in trendy Bucktown the best outdoor restaurant area isn't really, totally, 100-percent outdoors. **The Northside**'s walls retract but the ceiling stays put, so even in crappy weather you'll stay dry as the Gobi.

Isn't it romantic?... The mysterious "they" say that **Geja's Cafe** is the most romantic restaurant in town. It's dark, there's soft guitar music provided by a real musician, and dipping strawberries in chocolate fondue is, admittedly, sexy, but during the main part of the meal the noise of bubbling hot oil from the fondue pot on your table may remind you just a little too much of how goofy you thought fondue was back in the seventies. Up on North Halsted, **Oo-La-La!** is invitingly dark—the individual votives on each table cast a romantic glow on everyone's face—and the satisfying pastas leave you with a well-fed glow. Though the front room at **Sole Mio** in Lincoln Park is loud and raucous, there's a bunch of smaller rooms in the back with only a few tables each. With creamy walls, candlelight, and thou, what could be better?

Eating in the *other* gallery district... As River North real estate has moved younger art dealers selling edgier art to the Bucktown and Wicker Park neighborhoods, creative places to eat there have begun to sprout. The interior of **Soul Kitchen**, with its exotic art and brightly colored hanging lights and banners seems like a good backdrop for eating its Southern-style fare, while the swinging **Club Lucky** is where you might find a bunch of artists discussing deconstructionalism after a long day's gessoing.

Off the eaten track... If you find yourself in: Hyde Park, near the University of Chicago, try **Medici** for pizzas and other collegiate foods or **Dixie Kitchen & Bait Shop** for some good old-fashioned Southern home cookin'; in Little Italy head for **Francesca's on Taylor**, with crisp little pizzas, terrific Caesar salads, and a comfortable, woodsy, clubby atmosphere; in Pilsen checking out some of the many beautiful murals that dot the area, head for

Nueva Leon and chow down on authentic Mexican grub; in the no-man's-land of the Ukrainian Village try the unappetizingly named **Bite**, where the dichotomy between the seedy storefront atmosphere and sophisticated menu adds to the fun; in River West, inexpensive Southern home-cooking, served in a casual, cavernous space with big paintings of chickens lining the walls, is all that's needed to attract the hip-oisie to **Wishbone**'s seriously out-of-the-way location (out-of-the-way unless you work for the "Oprah Winfrey Show," since her studios are across the street).

Desserts to die for... There are sundaes with funny sounding names such as "Strike It Rich" (with toasted-almond ice cream and butterscotch topping) and "The Alcatraz Rock" (rocky road and vanilla ice cream armored with a shell of chocolate), but it's the buttery smooth ice cream and the deep, dark chocolates upon which **Ghiradelli Chocolate Shop & Soda Fountain**'s renown is based. Little Italy's **Mario's Italian Lemonade** is justifiably famous in Chicago, serving intensely flavored shaved ices. Unfortunately, it's only open May through October. If ice cream isn't your thing, head to River North and lap up **Brasserie Jo**'s sophisticated floating island or caramelized bread pudding. At **Wishbone**, in the neighborhood west of the Loop known as River West, comforting desserts such as rice pudding and apple pie, together with a great cup of coffee, hit the spot like nothing else.

Gay scenes... They're here, they're queer, and they eat at restaurants all over town, but a lot of gay people are sticking to places in the city's gayest neighborhood, known as Boys Town, north of Belmont Avenue, mostly along Halsted Street. Not as hip as of yore, **Angelina** still has long waits for a table, and with good reason: satisfying Italian food and lots of well-groomed guys who look like they're on first dates with each other. Go to **Ann Sather**, owned by gay community activist Tom Tunney, who bought the restaurant from the original Ann Sather and who has transformed it into a sort of community center, for gooey cinnamon rolls, great omelets all day and night long, and Swedish-inspired dinners. The cute-as-hell waiters at **Mia Francesca** make this hot trattoria definitely worth the long, long wait to get in (who cares about the food?). With its handpainted dark booths, sexy lighting, and heavy draperies, **Oo-La-La!** looks good, and in turn attracts a gayish, nightclubby crowd that looks equally good. The food is uneven (to be safe, order pasta), but that's beside the point.

Burgers... Decent burgers are a dime a dozen in most big urban areas, but the patties at **Medici** in Hyde Park, **Billy Goat Tavern** on Michigan Avenue (the legendary hangout of the muckrakers at the nearby *Chicago Tribune* and *Sun-Times*), the 1950s dinerlike **Johnny Rocket's**, and the swinging-singles, scene-stealing **P.J. Clarke's** are all considerable standouts. For the non–meat-eaters among you desperate to indulge in a burgerlike product, the veggie burger at **The Heartland Cafe** in Rogers Park is worth the schlepp to that far-North Side neighborhood.

In, right now... What does it mean to be in? Hot? The place to be? To many, the food, whether it's good or not, is secondary. It's the scene that matters, the buzz around town, the gossip-column mentions of Oprah-sightings that lend an air of chic. If the wait for a table is any judge, **Mia Francesca** is definitely in this category, as are French restaurants **Marché** and **Brasserie Jo**; the Southern food–serving **Soul Kitchen** in arty Wicker Park; Asian delights like the imperial looking **Ben Pao** and **Red Light** (the latter creates what it calls Asian "street food"); **Harry's Velvet Room**, where smoking cigars and swilling martoonis is a right of passage for many (especially, these days, for women), and **Bite** and **Iggy's**, two places that attract a crowd of artists, slackers, bikers, and other assorted fringe elements.

Dining 'n' dancing... At **Bossa Nova**, in Lincoln Park, the feisty tapas selection competes with equally loud and energetic music, mostly with a Latin beat, that may encourage you to dance off as many calories as you're putting on. Similarly, between huge, huge Mambo beers and platters of BBQ-sauce-dripping ribs, the jazz and Dixieland music at **Dick's Last Resort** encourages what comedian Steve Martin used to call "happy feet." If you're in the mood to watch dancing instead of actually doing it, at **Geja's Cafe**, a fondue restaurant where you cook your own dinner, flamenco dancers brighten weekend evenings.

The Index

$$$$$	over $50
$$$$	$40–$50
$$$	$30–$40
$$	$20–$30
$	under $20

Price categories reflect the cost of a three-course meal, not including drinks, taxes, and tip.

Angelina. Serving simple but tasty pastas, chicken, and fish dishes, this hip, two-room Italian restaurant is a neighborhood fave, but deserves a visit from outsiders as well, especially before hitting the nearby clubs.... *Tel 773/935–5933. 3561 N. Broadway, Red Line Addison el stop. $$*

Ann Sather. Homey, yes; cozy, not. But while this is supposed to be a Swedish restaurant, with Swedish potato sausage, Swedish meatballs, and sandwiches on limpa bread on the menu to prove it, it's the breakfasts-like-Mom-would-make that stand out (served all day and night long).... *Tel 773/ 348–2378, 929 W. Belmont Ave, Red Line Belmont el stop; tel 312/271–6677, 5207 N. Clark St., 22 bus, AE not accepted. $*

Bar Louie. Long 'n' thin, dark 'n' smoky—no, this is not Linda Evangelista we're talking about, but a loud, swinging bar-that-serves-Italian-food on the edge of River North, the once-hip gallery district. Ouch, are those bar stools uncomfortable.... *Tel 312/337–3313. 266 W. Chicago Ave., Brown Line Chicago el stop. $*

Ben Pao. OK, so it's definitely the best-looking Chinese restaurant in town—which for some is reason enough for a visit—and it serves funny drinks with umbrellas, but the food, despite exotic names like "chicken of good fortune" is just

OK.... *Tel 312/222–1888. 52 W. Illinois St., Red Line Grand & State el stop. Reservations recommended. $$*

Bice. Despite the pretension and high prices, this just-off-Michigan Avenue restaurant, the original of which is in Milan, has it all—including the regular Italian dishes you'd expect, like antipasto, and some you wouldn't, such as pasta in pesto with green beans and potatoes, and grilled quail wrapped in sage leaves and pancetta.... *Tel 312/664–1474. 158 E. Ontario St., Red Line Grand & State el stop. Reservations required. $$$$*

Big Bowl. Almost everything here is served in a big bowl. Got the gimmick? Actually, though, you'll be (excuse the pun) bowled over by the terrific dishes, from the grilled-vegetable soup with angel hair noodles to the ginger chicken, vegetable, and shrimp with roasted garlic. A new, second location caters to Rush Street night owls, open till midnight on weekends.... *Tel 312/787–8279, 159 1/2 W. Erie St., Red Line Grand & State el stop; tel 312/640–8888, 6 E. Cedar St., Red Line Clark & Division el stop. $*

Billy Goat Tavern. Within a block of both the *Sun-Times* and the *Chicago Tribune,* this dive—and that's a charitable description—is a media hangout, its walls covered with scores of sepia-tinted newspaper clippings. Greasy but delicious burgers are about the only thing worth eating.... *Tel 312/222–1525. 430 N. Michigan Ave., Red Line Grand & State el stop. No reservations. No credit cards. $*

Bite. Ignore the mangy dog that sometimes roams around this Ukrainian Village place (the Health Department does, apparently). Concentrate instead on the food, which is really good and really cheap. It's BYOB (or brave going into the rock club next door, which will sell you a beer or a glass of dreadful wine).... *Tel 773/395–2483. 1039 N. Western Ave., Blue Line Western el stop, transfer to 49 Western bus. $*

Bossa Nova. As swinging at the name implies, this cha-cha-cha nightclub features tapaslike meals (i.e., small) from around the world, from Spain to Asia to the American Southwest. Try the spicy "Suicide Chicken" or "Pasta from Hell," both of which get a three on the jalapeño-o-meter.... *Tel 773/248–4800. 1960 N. Clybourn Ave., Brown Line Armitage el stop. Reservations recommended. $$$*

Brasserie Jo. The kind of restaurant reviewers call *hot, hot, hot*. Of course there are loud, long waits, table-hopping yuppies pretending they're in Paris, and patrons who don't like to sit with their backs to the room because otherwise how will anyone know they're there? Ignore 'em and enjoy the over-the-top delicious traditional brasserie fare. Fun (homemade) beer concoctions, like beer and lemonade (it's better than it sounds).... *Tel 312/595–0800. 59 W. Hubbard St., Red Line Grand & State el stop. Reservations recommended. $$$*

Cafe Iberico. A real tapas bar—sprawling, raucous, loud, crowded, smoky.... *Tel 312/573–1510. 739 N. LaSalle St., Red Line Chicago & State el stop. AE not accepted. $$*

Chapulín. A beautiful room with murals by local artist Oscar Romero and dotted with Mexican folk art. Loud festive music and strong (but too small and expensive) drinks. The menu choices hail from the states of Puebla and Oaxaca and may include *quesadillas de cuitlacoche* (quesadillas stuffed with an exotic veggie called corn mushrooms), marinated quail, salmon in pumpkinseed sauce, and—you gotta try 'em—grilled grasshoppers (*chapulín*) or *escamoles* (ant eggs—no kidding), both of which taste and feel in your mouth like Grape Nuts, except they're hot.... *Tel 773/665–8677. 1962 N. Halsted St., Brown Line Armitage el stop. Reservations recommended. $$*

Club Lucky. The Italian food here—all the basics from minestrone to fried calimari to fettuccine Alfredo to chicken Vesuvio to cannoli—takes the proverbial back seat to the oh-so-swank scene. Low prices lure an artsy crowd.... *Tel 773/227–2300. 1824 W. Wabansia, Blue Line Damen el stop. Reservations recommended. $$*

Cullen's Bar & Grill. A raucous bar and grill, with a high tin ceiling and extravagant old-fashioned dark-wood bar, this Victorian-era looking place is actually less than a year old.... *Tel 773/975–0600. 3741 N Southport Ave., Brown Line Southport el stop. $*

Demon Dogs. A hot-dog joint under the el tracks next to De Paul University, serving reliably great bad-for-you food like wieners, Italian beef, polish sausage, and the like.... *Tel 312/281–2001. 944 W. Fullerton Ave., Dan Ryan line Fullerton el stop. $*

Dick's Last Resort. Frat living at its best (or worst, depending on your outlook): loud, raucous, everything chugged down with beer. You get to slobber over slabs o' ribs, messy chicken, and what they themselves call "squirty" crab legs; live music, mostly Dixieland jazz or the blues, is usually on tap too.... *Tel 312/836–7870. 435 E. Illinois St., Red Line Grand & State el stop, transfer to 29 Grand bus. $$*

Dish. The third or fourth restaurant to move into this tiny square space in almost as many years, this one (finally) seems to be a winner. The menu is more or less Mexican, with delicious fish Veracruzana and steak tacos, but every once in a while they'll throw in a special, like an incredibly good soft-shell crab/foccacia sandwich.... *Tel 773/549–8614. 3651 N. Southport Ave., Brown Line Southport el stop. $$$*

Dixie Kitchen & Bait Shop. Southern-style food in an obviously professionally art-directed "flea market" atmosphere, this restaurant near the University of Chicago in Hyde Park serves authentic johnnycakes, fried green tomatoes, crab fritters, gumbo, and country-fried steak. It's all bad for your heart, but oh-so-good for your soul.... *Tel 773/363-4943. 5225 S. Harper Ct., Red Line Garfield el stop. $$*

Francesca's on Taylor. In Little Italy, a big, clubby bilevel bustling place serving huge platters of red-sauced pastas, good fish and chicken dishes, terrific little pizzas. Loud, fun, and well suited for big parties. You have to valet park though, because the entire hood is permit parking only.... *Tel 312/829–2828. 1400 W. Taylor St., Blue Line UIC el stop. Reservations recommended. $$$*

Geja's Cafe. Is it dark and romantic or just dim and dreary? It depends on whom you're with, though this fondue restaurant has the rep as one of the most romantic restaurants in town. Also, you gotta cook your own grub—in hot oil.... *Tel 773/281–9101. 340 W. Armitage Ave., Brown Line Armitage el stop. Reservations recommended. $$$*

Ghiradelli Chocolate Shop & Soda Fountain. Justifiably famous, this cute soda shop just off Michigan Avenue is filled with bentwood chairs, small round marble-topped tables, old-fashioned posters, and a feeling of an era gone bye-bye: When you could eat a million-calorie dessert and not feel the need to check in with Jenny Craig.... *Tel 312/*

337–9330. 830 N. Michigan Ave., Red Line Chicago & State el stop. $

Gibsons Bar & Steakhouse. Near the Oak Street boutiques, this place is as subdued as the crowd isn't—huge booths, dark paneling, big ferns, good lighting. Try the steaks, of course—porterhouse to T-bone to sirloin to filet mignon—but don't skip well-prepared fish dishes either. Great baked potatoes, slathered in sour cream, naturally.... *Tel 312/266–8999. 1028 N. Rush St., Red Line Clark & Division el stop. Reservations recommended. $$$*

Gino's East. Really good pizza. Really long lines. But don't despair, they'll take your order while you wait for a table or booth in this dark, cavelike subterranean restaurant. Decades of patrons have carved their initials, witticisms, and a few unprintable bon mots into the wood tables. Makes for good reading.... *Tel 312/943–1124. 160 E. Superior St., Red Line Chicago & State el stop. No reservations. $$*

Giordano's. Arguably a step down from Uno and Gino's East, but you won't be sad if you have your deep-dish pizza here. There are other outlets around town; this is the flagship, so expect lines.... *Tel 312/951–0747. 730 N. Rush. Red Line Chicago el stop. DC not accepted. $$*

Gold Coast Dogs. Top-notch hot dogs and other indigenous fast foods.... *Tel 312/527–1222. 418 N. State St., Brown Line State & Lake el stop. No credit cards. $*

Hacienda Tecalitlan. With its 19th-century-inspired open-air courtyard and bubbling fountain, this cavernous Mexican restaurant looks (inside, at least) like it's been here forever, even though it was built just a year or so ago. The food—all the regulars you'd expect, like tortilla soup, plus a few you wouldn't, such as broiled quail—is just OK, and it's kind of expensive, but the atmosphere here is so charming, so truly Mexico City-ish that it's more than worth a visit.... *Tel 312/243–1166. 820 N. Ashland Ave., Blue Line Chicago el stop. Reservations recommended. $$$*

Harry's Velvet Room. Lushly outfitted, like Marrakesh meets Salvador Dali with a little Dean Martin thrown in for good measure. In other words, deep velvet swags, deep booths—the ambience is very Rat Pack, or at least trying to be.... *Tel 312/828–0770. 534 N. Clark St. Reservations recommended. $$*

The Heartland Cafe. Terrific semivegetarian restaurant with omelets and stir-frys, OK pasta, and, surprise, surprise, everything with tofu is a standout. The burgers are made from buffalo meat—not just any buffalo meat, but farm-raised buffalo meat.... *Tel 773/465–8005. 7000 N. Glenwood Ave., Red Line Morse el stop. $*

Hi Ricky. One of the better pan-Asian noodle shops that have sprung up around town like mushrooms, this place distinguishes itself with its hip interior and, in addition to the noodle end of things, its skewered satays. Service—such as it is—is either hurried or slowwwwww with no in-between.... *Tel 773/276–8300. 1852 W. North Ave., Red Line Damen el stop. $*

Home Run Inn. Tucked way out in a neighborhood on the Southwest Side you'll find what may be the best pizza in Chicago. Don't look for tourists here.... *Tel 312/247–9696. 4259 W. 31st St. Blue Line Cicero Ave. el stop, then CIcero Ave. Bus to 31st St. $*

Hong Min. Located in a bordering-on-seedy storefront in Chinatown, this is, nevertheless, one of the best Chinese restaurants in town. The service can be abrupt, but worth it to taste such great Cantonese and Mandarin dishes as steamed fish or barbecued pork in black bean and garlic sauce or chow foon noodles. BYOB.... *Tel 312/842–5026. 221 W. Cermak Rd., Red Line Cermak el stop. AE not accepted. $$*

Iggy's. So, you walk past the projects across the street, scoot by the motorcycles parked out front, whoosh through the heavy black velvet drapery just inside the front door, all to be accosted by one of the smokiest joints in town. That's the bad part; the good part, however, is really good. Like the food—mostly grilled this and that and a terrific salad Niçoise.... *Tel 312/829–4449. 700 N. Milwaukee Ave., Blue Line Chicago el stop. $$*

Italian Village. Actually composed of three Italian restaurants under one roof, the Italian Village has been here in the Loop since 1927. Busy at the pretheater rush. Take your choice of chi-chi (Vivière), seafood (La Cantina), or traditional small-town Italy (The Village). You can't lose.... *Tel 312/332–7005. 77 W. Monroe., Red Line Monroe & State el stop. Reservations required. $$–$$$*

Johnny Rocket's. Red and black and white all over, with mini-jukeboxes at each booth–you get the picture. Don't stray much beyond burgers, fries, malts, and shakes at this transplant from L.A.'s Melrose Boulevard, and you'll do fine. Kids love it here, and the corner windows make for good people-watching.... *Tel 312/337–3900. 901 N. Rush St., Red Line Chicago & State el stop. No credit cards. $*

Korean Restaurant. A plain-as-day storefront in an out-of-the-way North Side hood you've really got to want to go to. Still, the food is weirdly tasty and definitely exotic: try the *bibim naeng myon* (buckwheat noodles in hot sauce), *bibim bap* (rice with meat, vegetables, egg and red sauce), grilled mackerel, ox blood soup.... *Tel 773/878–2095. 2659 W. Lawrence Ave., Brown Line Damen el stop. $$*

Leona's Pizzeria. A lotta food at low prices: huge servings of typical red-sauce pastas come with a salad and warm bread big enough for a meal themselves. Thick-crust pizzas, thin-crust pizzas, stuffed pizzas—it's all here, as are long lines at peak hours, hosts who wear Madonna-like headsets to communicate with one another, and a college-pizza-joint-on-steroids sort of atmosphere.... *Tel 773/327–8861. 3215 N. Sheffield Ave., Red Line Belmont el stop. $$*

Leo's Lunchroom. Don't be fooled by the divelike looks of this tiny storefront restaurant. It's not only as if a trained chef just happens to be in the kitchen of a greasy spoon—there is a trained chef here, turning out imaginative, eclectic cuisine.... *Tel 773/276–6509. 1809 W. Division., Blue Line Division el stop. No reservations. No credit cards. $$*

Marché. Yes, there's paillard of this and a gratinée of that on the menu at this grandly decorated bistro, but the chef here uses French cuisine merely as inspiration. Try the aromatic couscous with grilled vegetables, the *haricots verts* with fennel and tomato, or any of the spectacular desserts.... *Tel 312/226–8399. 833 W. Randolph St., Green Line Clinton & Lake el stop. Reservations recommended. $$$$*

Mario's Italian Lemonade. Open only from late May through October, this teensy-weensy shack sells some of the best flavored Italian shaved ice this side of Venice. Long lines on hot summer nights, but after all that standing and sweating, the ices taste even better.... *No phone. 1070 W. Taylor St., Blue Line UIC Halsted el stop. $*

Medici. A short distance from the University of Chicago, this college and neighborhood hangout serves great burgers, natch, as well as salads, pizzas, and beer.... *Tel 773/667-7394. 1327 E. 57th St. South Shore Metra 57th St. el stop. $*

The Melrose Restaurant. Yeccch. To be fair, some people like the greasy diner food here and occasionally a wacky waitress who wears neon earrings and funny makeup gets written about in the paper, but really, there are only two distinguishing factors at work here: It's open around the clock, so the après-club scene can be fun, and in summer the outdoor cafe is one of the best people-watching spots in town.... *Tel 773/327-2060. 3233 N. Broadway, Red Line Belmont el stop. $$*

Mia Francesca. About as sizzling as sizzling restaurants in Chicago get, this trattoria has managed to stay hot thanks to moderate prices and consistently good food. The menu changes daily, but may include Portabello-mushroom pizza, roasted red snapper, and a mélange of great pastas—there isn't a bad dish to be had. Oprah occasionally eats here, but because reservations aren't taken, she has other people endure the two-hour waits for her.... *Tel 773/281-3310. 3311 N. Clark St., Red Line Addison el stop. No reservations. AE not accepted. $$*

The Northside. The first yuppie bar/restaurant to invade funky Bucktown, though thankfully it didn't start a trend. Good sandwiches, burgers, salads. Lotsa people in their college sweatshirts, reminiscing about the big game.... *Tel 773/384-3555. 1635 N. Damen Ave., Blue Line Damen el stop. $$*

Nueva Leon. Should you find yourself in the Mexican neighborhood called Pilsen, this authentic diner is very worth a stopover. If you've got a craving for chimichanga, cheese-oozing enchiladas, guacamole-seeping burritos, and lard-leaking refried beans, this is the place to fulfill it. Locals eat here, which is always a good sign, and it's open way late on weekends. BYOB.... *Tel 312/421–1517. 1515 W. 18th St., Blue Line 18th St. el stop. $*

Oo-La-La! Great looking place, with its handpainted dark booths, sexy lighting, and heavy draperies. The food at times is terrific and at other times merely OK. The pastas are your best bet, from the plain-as-day pasta pomodoro, which is too simple to screw up, to the *fettuccine al sapori forti* (pasta with pine nuts, raisins, and garlic), which when it's good is really good. Fish is sometimes way overcooked.... *Tel 773/935–7708. 3335 N. Halsted St., Red Line Belmont el stop. Reservations required. $$*

Paladino's. Big, great-looking (though very loud) two-story restaurant serving huge portions of so-so pastas and chicken dishes; the banana crème brûlée, however, is worth a trip here; great cityscape views from the second floor.... *Tel 312/455–1400. 832 W. Randolph St., Green Line Clinton & Lake el stop. Reservations recommended. $$*

The Pepper Lounge. Martinis-to-die-for and other swank cocktail concoctions are the leitmotif here, though the food—mostly pastas and grilled fish and chicken dishes—are awfully good.... *Tel 312/665–7377. 3441 N. Sheffield Ave., Red Line Addison el stop. Reservations required. $$$*

Pizzeria Uno. Basically the same as Gino's East.... *Tel 312/321–1000. 29 E. Ohio St., Red Line Grand & State el stop. $*

P.J. Clarke's. Swinging singles—overgrown frat boys; too-tan, itsy-bitsy women with big hair; guys who drive Corvettes for dubious reasons; and women who say "like" a lot—cram into this tin-ceilinged bar-and-grill for juicy burgers, great Caesar salads, and even spaghetti.... *Tel 312/664–1650. 1204 N. State Pkwy., Red Line Clark & Division el stop. $$*

Portillo's. Amid all the theme restaurants of River North, there's this theme restaurant, which happens to serve pretty good hot dogs, Italian beefs, and other Chicago-type food.... *Tel 312/587–8910. 100 W. Division. Howard Line Grand el stop. $*

Ranalli's off Rush. A simple late-night pizza and pasta joint with black-and-white photos of old-time Chicago and balcony views of the bar-hopping scene.... *Tel 312/440–*

7000. 24 W. Elm St., Red Line Clark & Division el stop. D not accepted. $

Red Light. "Street food" from the Pacific Rim (i.e., Hong Kong, Shanghai, Penang, Singapore). Very chic crowd (too chic for some tastes). One of the city's newest.... *Tel 312/226–2232. 820 W. Randolph St., Green Line Clinton & Lake el stop. Reservations recommended. $$$*

Ritz-Carlton Cafe. An expensive way to end the day, but if you're bored with all the funky places you've been to, this posh hotel cafe is just the antidote: lavish burgers with fries, vegetarian stew, turkey pot pie, and even a dense osso bucco.... *Tel 312/266–1000. 160 E. Pearson St., Red Line Chicago & State el stop. $$$*

Russian Tea Time. Red leather banquettes, Russian music, and a waitstaff barking Russian at one another while they move through the very close together tables serving authentic borscht, stuffed cabbage, and many other dishes with lots of consonants in their names will transport you to post-Soviet Russia, specifically Uzbekistan, from which the owners hail. But beware, Russian food is not known for its healthy attributes and some of it is exceptionally stick-to-your-ribs.... *Tel 312/360–0000. 77 E. Adams St., Red Line Monroe & State el stop. Reservations recommended. $$$*

Sole Mio. The type of well-lighted, loud, bustling place in which Woody Allen would film something. Great puffy pizzas with caramelized onions, seafood risotto, grilled salmon, pepper steak with a huge mound of fries that looks like someone left Carol Channing's wig on your plate. The bartender (endearingly) has a heavy hand. Lots of rooms, but the front room is the swingingest....*Tel 773/477–5858. 917 W. Armitage St., Brown Line Armitage el stop. Reservations recommended. $$$$*

Soul Kitchen. The busboys wear T-shirts that say "Loud food and spicy music," which just about sums up this Southern-food, artsy hangout in Bucktown.... *Tel 312/342–9742. 1574 N. Milwaukee Ave., Blue Line Damen el stop. No reservations. $$$*

Strega Nona. Bustling (i.e., very loud) Italian restaurant that cleverly avoids the standards. Instead, unusual pastas tossed with odd combinations of vegetables and meats, such as green-tea noodles with grilled shrimp and toasted sesame seeds or flower-shaped gigli with lobster and vodka sauce.... *Tel 773/244–0990. 3747 N. Southport Ave., Brown Line Southport el stop. No reservations. $$$*

SuperDawg. As you cruise up Milwaukee Avenue, you'll see a big wiener wearing a loincloth and heaving a barbell as an adoring girl wiener looks on. Turn your car into the driveway, order a couple of dogs and go large on the fries—they're terrific.... *Tel 312/763–0660. 6363 N. Milwaukee Ave. Blue Line Jefferson Park el stop. $*

Tempo. A diner, nothing more than a diner, but the French toast is puffy and good, the eggs are runny and satisfying, the burgers aren't so bad, either, and the tuna salad is A-OK, if you're a creamy tuna–lover as opposed to a chunky tuna–lover. The real draw, though, are the late hours and the outdoor eating area which overlooks the passing just-off-Michigan Avenue parade.... *Tel 312/943–4373. 1 E. Chestnut St., Red Line Chicago & State el stop. $*

The Third Coast. Hot location a block off Michigan Avenue and good inexpensive food that people actually want to eat (home-baked scones oozing raspberries, fresh-tasting eggs, really good salad Niçoise, and, hallelujah, perfectly fine coffee—espresso, etc.). No wonder it's one of the neighborhood's most popular hangouts.... *Tel 312/664–7225. 29 E. Delaware Pl., Red Line Chicago & State el stop. $* A second location—same name, different owner, slightly different menu—is open 24 hours.... *Tel 312/649–0730. 1260 N. Dearborn Pkwy., Red Line Clark & Division el stop. $*

Tin-Yen. The walls are green, the carpeting is green, the booths are green—even the food is.... Actually, the Cantonese food at the Chinatown place—from the crunchy wide rice noodles to the crabs in garlic sauce to the overflowing portion of great-tasting sweet-and-sour soup—really hits the spot. And boy, is it cheap.... *Tel 312/842–7156. 2242 S. Wentworth Ave., Red Line Cermak el stop. $*

Trattoria Gianni. Comfortable, modern trattoria that looks like it's been around since, well, the late 1970s. Good, solid food—pastas, Caesar salad, antipasto—you get the picture. Near a few theaters, so it's really crowded before curtain time and then totally clears out.... *Tel 312/266–1976. 1711 N. Halsted Ave., Red Line North & Clybourn el stop. Reservations recommended. $$$*

Twilight. Picture Bette Davis. Picture her walking into this small storefront joint in the scruffy-but-starting-to-get-hip Ukrainian Village neighborhood, looking around, blowing a puff of cigarette smoke in your face and saying, "What a dump." She'd be right, too, except that the food here is anything but dumpy: grilled fish, garlicky chicken, fish wrapped and grilled in banana leaves. BYOB—and they serve it in whatever's handy, like coffee mugs and juice glasses (were you expecting stemware?).... *Tel 773/862–8757. 1924 W. Division St., Blue Line Division el stop. $$*

The Wiener Circle. Burgers are better than the dogs here, and the fries are some of the best in town. There's really nowhere to eat except at the few icky wood picnic tables out front, where you can sit in the wake of the carbon monoxide spewed from passing buses.... *Tel 312/477–7444. 2622 N. Clark St., Red Line Fullerton el stop. No credit cards. $*

Wishbone. At this hip, casual restaurant, Southern home-cooking, such as pan-fried chicken or house specialty hoppin' John (black-eyed peas over rice with cheddar, scallions, and tomatoes) comes with two sides—the yams and spinach are the best. Of course, they also serve great pecan pie and pretty good grits (that is, if you're disposed to even like grits).... *Tel 312/850–2663. 1001 W. Washington St., Green Line Clinton & Lake el stop. $$*

Yoshi's Cafe. Owner Yoshi Katsumara has taken what was once one of Chicago's fanciest restaurants and recently doubled its size and rejiggered the menu from top to bottom. Now a cafe serving everything from individual-sized pizzas to roasted fish to marinated tofu steaks to salad Niçoise, the looking-for-a-bargain crowds have descended.... *Tel 773/248–6160. 3257 N. Sheffield Ave., Red Line Belmont el stop. Reservations recommended. $$*

down
and
dirty

Bulletin boards... Study flyers and postcards dropped off at **Tower Records** (2301 N. Clark St.) or **Untitled/Aero** (2701 N. Clark St.), a hip-hop and raver clothing shop in Lincoln Park, or any trendy shop in Lake View or Wicker Park, for club discounts and clues about the underground party scene.

Festivals and special events...

January: New and emerging local choreographers and dance companies performing in a variety of styles—African, modern, tap, experimental, and more—show off their stuff over two weekends in **Chicago's Next Dance Festival** (tel 773/784–6735; various theaters).

February: A bunch of small, out-there Chicago theater groups banded together years go to throw their own theater festival (see August below); a cold-weather outgrowth is **Rhino in Winter** (tel 773/327–6666, 2827 N. Lincoln Ave.), a monthlong confab of mostly solo performers and other performance work at Lunar Cabaret and Full Moon Cafe.

March: The **Spring Festival of Dance** (tel 312/629–8696) brings out many of the city's dance companies for multiple Chicago performances through early June. The mayor's still named Daley and the Chicago River continues to bleed Kelly green on or around March 17 for the downtown **St. Patrick's Day Parade** (tel 312/744–3315; Dearborn St. at Wacker Dr.); that evening, expect the city's pubs and taverns to be crawling with people wearing goofy foam shamrocks on their heads. The **Women in the Director's Chair International Film and Video Festival** (tel 773/281–4988; various theaters) is a four-day presentation of mostly short works and a few feature films from, you guessed it, women directors.

April: The 10-day **Chicago Latino Film Festival** (tel 312/431–1330; various theaters) screens more than 100 movies, short films, and videos from Latin America, Portugal, Spain, the United States, and other countries, in their original language with English subtitles. All month, the lakefront lights up after dark with the cooking fires of fisherfolk during **smelt season** (tel 312/814–2070).

May: Like the leafing of trees and the budding of flowers in Chicago, the annual revival of the **Buckingham Fountain Color Light Show** (tel 312/747–2474; Grant Park, Congress Pkwy. and Lake Shore Dr.) is a hopeful and magnificent sight. The waterworks flow through October. Chicagoans converge on Grant Park for the first of the summer's big music festivals, the **Viva! Chicago Latin Music Festival** (tel 312/744–3315; Petrillo Music Shell, Grant Park). Bailiwick Repertory presents a summer-long festival of lesbian and gay plays, performance art, comedy, and cabaret during its **Pride Performance Series** (tel 773/883–1090; 1229 W. Belmont Ave.). By far one of the more colorful conventions held each year in this convention town is **International Mr. Leather Weekend** (tel 800/545–6753), which draws thousands of cowskin-clad gay men (and a small number of leather Lizzies) for a leather-goods fair, big parties, and the crowning of a new titleholder over Memorial Day weekend. More than 150 international dealers of contemporary art set up gallery spaces midmonth at Navy Pier for one of the biggest art shows of the year, **Art Chicago** (tel 312/587–3300), a six-day exposition.

June: Like pioneers staking their claim in an Oklahoma land run, Chicagoans vie for patches of grass in Grant Park during some of its famous free summer concerts—the **Chicago Blues Festival** on the first weekend in June or the last in May; the **Chicago Gospel Festival** on the second weekend in June; and the **Chicago Country Music Festival** around the last weekend (for all three events, tel 312/744–3315). All performances extend into the evening and are staged at the Petrillo Band Shell at Columbus Dr. and Jackson Blvd. Look to the same stage for the **Grant Park Music Festival** (tel 312/742–4763), a free series of classical, jazz, and pop concerts beginning midmonth that runs through August. On the North Shore, the Chicago Symphony Orchestra opens its summer season at the open-air **Ravinia Festival** (tel 773/728–4642; Lake-Cook and Green Bay roads, Highland Park), which also presents jazz, country, and pop artists through September. On the last weekend of the month, Chicagoans crowd into Grant Park to feed their faces with chow from dozens of the city's restaurants at the 10-day **Taste of Chicago** (tel 312/744–3315), one of the biggest summer festivals that stays in full swing until 9pm. **Gay and Lesbian Pride Month** (tel 773/348–8243) gives rise to a panoply of concerts, lectures, dances, readings, and dozens of other special events throughout June, culminating in the annual parade, which naturally jump-starts an evening of revelry at the city's lesbian and gay bars. Edgy works from 30 different theater groups from around the world are offered up over two weeks during the recently launched **Chicago Fringe and Buskers Festival** (tel 773/327–5588; various theaters).

July: Huge crowds turn out on July 3 for the **Independence Day Concert and Fireworks Show** (tel 312/744–3315; Petrillo Music Shell, Grant Park), getting their annual fix of the Grant Park Symphony performing Tchaikovsky's *1812 Overture*. **The World's Largest Block Party** (tel 312/782–6171; Adams and Des Plaines streets) draws partyers the third weekend of July to the streets around the downtown Old St. Patrick's Church for food, drink, and live rock and blues bands. Thousands of amateur bicyclists traverse 25 miles of the North Side and lakefront on the **L.A.T.E. (Long After Twilight Ends) Ride** (tel 773/918–7433), a benefit on the second Saturday of the month for Friends of the Parks. Riders rendezvous toward sunrise for breakfast at Buckingham Fountain. Late in the month, a flotilla of illuminated tall ships, sailboats, and other vessels gather in Monroe Harbor for one of the city's oldest summer traditions, **Venetian Night** (tel 312/744–3315); the boat parade is followed by fireworks. What may be the country's largest Mexican neighborhood festival, the 3-day **Fiesta del Sol** (tel 312/666–2663, Blue Island from 18th St. to Cermak) goes late into the night the last weekend in July with food, arts and crafts vendors, carnival rides, and music and dancing. A good buzz is had by all at the **Chicago Peace and Music Festival** (tel 312/252–9150; Humboldt Park, North and California avenues), a mini-Woodstock of bands and vendors the last weekend of the month. The **Independent Label Festival** (tel 312/341–9112) showcases 150 rock and alternative bands at a dozen clubs in the city during the weekend-long music-industry convention at the end of the month.

August: Early in August, the mother of all summer street festivals, **Northalsted Market Days** (tel 773/868–3010), packs Halsted Street between Belmont Avenue and Addison Street with food and crafts vendors, some pretty decent bands, and a colorful uninhibited, mostly gay crowd from all over the Midwest. Geared to children and families, the three-day **Magic City Festival** (tel 312/744–1612) midmonth presents nearly 250 performances by singers, dancers, storytellers, mimes, puppeteers, and others on stages throughout Navy Pier. Beginning midmonth, the eclectic **Rhinoceros Theater Festival** (tel 773/327–6666, Lunar Cabaret and Full Moon Cafe) stages six weeks of full-length plays, solo performance pieces, and musical shows from Chicago's avant-garde.

September: The city's cultural heavy hitters, the **Lyric Opera of Chicago** (tel 312/332–2244) and the **Chicago Symphony Orchestra** (tel 312/435–6666), inaugurate their new seasons. The art-season opener floods galleries in the **River North Gallery District** (tel 312/649–0064) on the first Friday evening after Labor Day, with free-loading art gawkers looking to binge on free wine and cheese. Another of the biggest art events of the year, **Around the Coyote** (tel 773/342–6777) on four days in early September offers the public a peek into the studios of hundreds of artists in the Wicker Park/Bucktown neighborhood, said to be home to the second largest concentration of artists in the country. This event is accompanied by concerts; a fashion show; theatrical, dance, and poetry performances; and other special events. The **Chicago Jazz Festival** (tel 312/744–3315) brings big-name artists to the stage at the Petrillo Music Shell in Grant Park for three days early in the month or at the end of August. A Chicago institution, the century-old Berghoff restaurant transforms Adams Street between Dearborn and State into a beer garden for bratwurst, the brewery's fall amber ale, and oompah bands midmonth for four days during **Octoberfest** (tel 312/427-3170). Yes, it's in September. Don't ask.

October: A somewhat second-tier stop on the celluloid circuit, the **Chicago International Film Festival** (tel 312/644–3456; Music Box Theater, Fine Arts, and other cinemas) schedules more than 100 films from 30 countries, as well as lectures by directors, actors, and producers over two or so weeks. Kids get their own movies too: The **Chicago International Children's Film Festival** (tel 773/281–9075), the largest of its kind in North America, presents a few of its 130 film and video offerings from 35 countries before bedtime during its 10-day run. **Dance Chicago** (tel 773/935–6860; Athenaeum Theatre and others), the city's fall dance festival, showcases emerging Chicago-based dance troupes, choreographers, and performance art in a six-week run that gives audiences the chance to sample several companies on one bill.

November: On the second weekend, the **Chicago Humanities Festival** (tel 312/422–5580), held at the city's major educational and cultural institutions, explores philosophical themes like "birth and death" with lectures, performances, and debates by leading scholars, writers, singers, and policy makers. The **Chicago Lesbian and Gay International Film Festival** (tel 773/384–5533, Music Box Theater and Chicago Filmmakers) showcases about 100 flicks from North America, Europe, and elsewhere, in a 10-day run. The merchants of North Michigan Avenue hope for some trickle-down business from the hundreds of thousands of people who line the street for the **Magnificent Mile Lights Festival** (tel 312/642–3570; from Oak St. to the Chicago River), a parade held the weekend before Thanksgiving that culminates with the ignition of twinkly white lights along the tree-lined street. The holiday spirit gets another lift with the city's **Christmas Tree Lighting** downtown in Daley Plaza the day after Thanksgiving (tel 312/744–3315). The giraffes haven't been forced to wear Santa hats yet, but Lincoln Park Zoo is strewn with thousands of colorful illuminated displays during the **ZooLights Festival** (tel 312/742–2000; 2200 N. Cannon Dr.), Thanksgiving through Christmas. The event features choral groups, theater and dance performances, special activities for children, and a visit from Santa.

December: You've got two *Nutcrackers* to choose from during the holidays: the long-standing Chicago Tribune charity benefit production featuring international dancers and 100 local children (tel 312/791–6000; Arie Crown Theatre, McCormick Place, 23rd St. and Lake Shore Dr.) or the renowned show by the New York transplant **Joffrey Ballet of Chicago** (tel 312/739–0120; call for location). The Prairie Avenue House Museums (the city's oldest surviving building), the 1836 Clarke House, and the 1887 Glessner House are decorated in period holiday decorations for two weekends of **Holiday Candlelight Tours** (tel 312/326–1480; reservations recommended).

Hotlines... The **Mayor's Office of Special Events Hotline**, tel 312/744–3370; **Chicago Music Alliance** (for information relating to classical concerts and operas), tel 312/987–1123; **Concert Line** (for all the main venues, mostly rock), tel 312/666–6667; **Chicago Dance Coalition Hotline**, tel 312/419–8383; **Jazz** hotline, tel 312/427–3300; **Movie Phone**, tel 312/444–FILM; **WXRT-FM Hotline**

(for information on rock, blues, and folk concerts, shows, and festivals), tel 773/481–9978.

Newspapers and magazines... The city's main alternative paper, the ***Reader***, gets much of its heft from voluminous reviews, listings, and ads for concerts, performing arts, bars and nightclubs, and other nightlife attractions. Published on Thursday afternoons, the free tabloid also prides itself on providing the city's most complete theater coverage, reviewing even the most obscure productions. More extensive profiles and reviews are carried in the ***Chicago Tribune***'s daily arts section and its "Friday" entertainment pullout, where the "After Hours" column highlights offbeat evening haunts; the competing ***Sun-Times*** has Friday "Weekend Plus" and Sunday "Showcase" sections. The *Sun-Times* isn't mandatory reading—the *Trib* is more comprehensive and has better critics. ***Chicago*** magazine, the city's slick monthly, is worth a look for its rather straightforward capsule reviews of the city's best restaurants, as well as listings of cultural events and performances.

Online information... Before you get to town, do a little Internet noodling through a few helpful Chicago-related sites on the World Wide Web. Two comprehensive sites with information and links to a variety of local interests are the **Chicago Office of Tourism** (http://www.ci.chi.il.us/tourism) and one maintained by the **Chicago Public Library** (http://cpl.lib.uic.edu/004chicago/004chicago.html). A few other sites are: **Blues clubs and concerts**, http://nitescape.com/chicago/blues/; **Jazz clubs and concerts**, http://www.tezcat.com/~jmiles/index.html; **Classical music**, http://nuinfo.nwu.edu/ev-chi/music/; **Rock concerts**, http://www.tezcat.com/~andy/shows/; **Theater**, http://nuinfo.nwu.edu/ev-chi/theaters/.

Look to the entertainment pullout section in ***N'Digo***, a free bimonthly tabloid, for an African-American perspective; ***¡Exito!*** is a Spanish-language weekly that keeps tabs on Latino-related live music and happenings. The city's predominant lesbian and gay newspaper, ***Windy City Times***, offers its own spin on gay and nongay cultural events. The irreverent gay freebie ***Gab***, available at many bars and stores in Lake View, dishes the local gay and lesbian party circuit.

Parking... Parking in Chicago is easy if you opt for a lot, hard if you depend on your parking karma to divine a spot. There are numerous city-operated downtown garages close to some of the city's major attractions, including: **Grant Park North**, Monroe Street at Michigan Avenue (tel 312/742–7530); **Grant Park South**, Michigan Avenue at Van Buren Street (tel 312/747–2519); **Navy Pier**, 600 E. Grand Avenue (tel 312/595–PIER); and **Soldier Field**, 14th Street and Lake Shore Drive (tel 312/747–2766).

The parking problem is increasingly the bane of life in neighborhoods such as Lincoln Park and Lake View. Small neighborhood lots are common, and valet parking serves many restaurants, nightclubs, and bars (which starts to look pretty good after your second or third loop around the block). Such services start at about $6, which is not all that expensive if you can split it among a few passengers. Unless you want to risk a ticket, watch carefully for parking restrictions posted on neighborhood side streets. Much of the north side is annoyingly off-limits to nonresident cars after 5pm; the same goes for the area around Wrigley Field during night games.

Phone facts... Once upon a time, Chicago's equivalent of New York's bridge-and-tunnel crowd was neatly referred to as "708ers," getting the epithet from the area code shared by folks outside the city limits. Now the suburbs have been divided into a zillion different area codes, and even urbanites are being pitted against each other with two area codes in the city. It's all very confusing. The classic **312 area code** applies to people working or living in the Loop—what Chicagoans call downtown—north to North Avenue, south to 35th Street, and west to Western Avenue, while the rest of the city gets the newfangled, and some think rather inelegant, **773 area code**. (All phone numbers listed in this book reflect the new area code arrangement.) Most pay phones cost 35 cents here, even for directory assistance calls.

Public transportation... The Chicago Transit Authority operates seven el lines and more than 200 bus routes. Fares are $1.50 and an extra 30 cents for a transfer, which entitles you to two connections to a bus or el line within the next couple of hours. There are reduced fares for children, seniors, and people with disabilities. A CTA hotline (tel 312/836–7000; TDD 800/439–2202), which operates until 1am, can help you figure out how to get to where you want to go.

The **el** (for elevated, even though one of the lines runs as a subway downtown) extends to the far South Side, north to Evanston and the North Shore, and west to Oak Park; the lines are identified by color (Red Line, Blue Line, etc.). Pay either at a station, or aboard the train if the station ticket booth is closed. But be warned: The CTA doesn't accept bills larger than $20—a major pain when you've just left the ATM and are rushing to make a train. Packs of 10 tokens are sold at a slight discount at currency exchanges and major grocery chains like Jewel and Dominick's. El platforms are covered but still open to the elements, making them miserable places to stand on a cold, windy night. It helps somewhat that they're equipped with heat lamps. Trains run every six to 15 minutes during the early evening, but after midnight they can be as infrequent as once an hour. The cash-strapped CTA has been threatening to stop operating trains all night, but for the moment most lines operate 24 hours a day—a notable exception being the Brown Line (don't say we didn't warn you). Check the schedule to make sure there'll be a train at the station you need at the end of your night. Only a handful of the el stations on each line have elevators—contact the CTA (tel 800/606-1282) about special services for disabled passengers.

Just about every major street in the city has a **bus line**. Chicago is built on a grid of east-west and north-south streets (with a few diagonals, like Clark, Milwaukee, and Lincoln avenues, to mix things up), and bus drivers follow their prescribed routes back and forth, back and forth, back and forth, all night long. Fun job, huh? Drivers sometimes call out stops, but it's often difficult to understand their mumbling. However, they're usually pretty helpful if you need help figuring out where to get off. Located every couple of blocks, stops are marked by blue-and-white signs identifying the routes. Buses accept only exact change (including dollar bills). They run about every five to 20 minutes (depending on the route), and every half hour overnight. Most of the bus lines run until late evening; the major ones that go all night are marked with an owl symbol. Buses are accessible to people with disabilities and equipped with lifts.

Radio... Tune into **WBEZ (91.5 FM)**, the local National Public Radio affiliate, for erudite discussions of the latest cultural happenings, during arts programs aired Friday and Saturday afternoons. A big backer of local music, **WXRT (93.1 FM)** clues its enlightened yuppie listeners into rock, folk, and pop concerts and happenings around town; while **WGCI (107.5 FM)** has the lowdown on R&B and dance acts; and **WKQX (101.1 FM)** satisfies its Lollapaloozoid listeners with news of alternative acts.

Safety tips... You can explore much of Chicago without turning into a crime statistic by using simple common sense. Be alert, pay attention to where you are (and know where that is), and avoid walking around alone after a few drinks at two o'clock in the morning. There's safety in numbers on North Michigan Avenue and River North, where tons of people roam the streets at night, but going out to bars or theaters in Lincoln Park and Lake View often means passing down quiet neighborhood streets. It's always safer to stick to better-illuminated major thoroughfares. Many of the hipper spots are found in far-flung reaches of the city, notably Wicker Park, a gentrifying area that's still a bit rough around the edges.

When taking the train or bus late at night, it's a good idea to travel with a group; el platforms and subway stops can be spookily deserted after hours. When you get on the el, consider sitting near the conductor.

Chicago police cars cruise the streets in white Chevy Caprices with blue lettering; you can also reach the police by dialing **911** from any telephone. There are also precinct offices smack in the middle of a couple of major nightlife areas: at Halsted and Addison streets near Wrigley Field, and at Chicago and Clark streets near the River North/ Ontario Street restaurant and nightclub corridor. The **Pink Angels** (tel 312/871–PINK), a gay version of the Guardian Angels, patrol the Halsted area on weekends watching for potential bashers.

Taxis... If you've got the money to spend, taxicabs are perhaps the best way to get around Chicago at night. They're more convenient than public transportation, take you right to your doorstep, and are pretty economical on short hops. Street parking can be nearly impossible downtown and near any place you want to visit at night; even locals will hail cabs to preserve a precious parking spot for their car.

Cabs are plentiful in much of the city, though harder to find as you get farther from downtown and the busiest nightlife and theater strips. Often you only have to step to the curb and a cab will pass by within a few minutes. Cabs use a light on top to indicate whether they're available for a ride; if the light is off, they've already got a customer or are off duty. It always helps to have a pretty good idea of where you want to go; don't be surprised if your driver doesn't know the way or isn't familiar with your destination. Drivers here are relatively pleasant, but as in any other big city, you occasionally do get a driver who needs a little coaching on his manners or who drives like he's rushing you to the hospital when you're in no hurry at all.

Fares are determined by distance and waiting time. Within the city limits, meters start at $1.50 when you step into the cab and accrue $1.20 for each additional mile. A 50-cent surcharge is tacked on for each additional passenger over age 12. You may consider making a reservation for a taxi; call **Yellow Cab** (tel 312/TAXI-CAB) or **Checker** (tel 312/CHECKER).

Tickets... In general, it's pretty easy to see smaller off-Loop shows simply by leaving your name on the theater's answering machine; your place usually will be guaranteed if you show up at least 15 minutes before showtime, and someone will return your call if they're already sold out. Larger theaters guarantee seats by taking plastic over the phone, though you might want to save on the minimal service charge by stopping by the box office.

If you're staying at a hotel, your concierge can help find seats to "sold-out" sporting or theatrical events. While they may be able to get their hands on tickets for hard-to-get shows by going through their favorite ticket brokers, be prepared to pay a premium. Check with the concierge about schmoozing a seat at a hot restaurant that's booked; the better hotels often have the clout to open up a table. The downtown **Marshall Field's** (tel 312/781–4483, 111 N. State St., open store hours) has a concierge desk of sorts: the store's Visitor Service desk, located on the basement level, near the wine and stationery sections (the State and Randolph side), where the staff will make free suggestions about sightseeing trips, help with restaurant reservations, and call around for ticket reservations.

Like a loud, unruly neighbor, you don't like **Ticketmaster**; you just live with it. They're often the only source for all sorts of concert, theater, and sports tickets. Yes, this is aggravating, but you very well might have to deal with them and their generous surcharges during your visit. You can charge tickets on a credit card by phone (tel 312/559–1212) or pay with cash only at one of their outlets, located at Carson Pirie Scott & Co. (1 S. State St.) and Tower Records (2301 N. Clark St. and 214 S. Wabash Ave.). Alternatively, try one of the Hot Tix locations (see below).

The Yellow Pages lists dozens of ticket brokers; you can turn to one if you're pressed for time and don't mind shelling out the bucks. All are required to be state-licensed, but if you have any doubts, try either **Tower Ticket Service** (tel 312/454–1300) or **Gold Coast Tickets** (tel 312/644–6446), both reputable services. Order by phone with your credit card (be prepared to absorb fees based on availability, demand, and so on), and your tickets can be delivered either that day or the next. Less legitimate, and a misdemeanor in Illinois, is selling scalped tickets. But take a walk around Wrigley Field or the United Center on a game day and you'll see that the law hasn't exactly driven the illegal ticket trade underground. Be wary of what you buy on the street—you'll feel like a rube if you buy tickets to last week's game.

Several theaters sell cut-rate tickets at the box office on the night of a performance, and many discount prices for students, children, and senior citizens. Otherwise, your best money-saving bet may be **Hot Tix** (tel 312/977–1755), run by the nonprofit League of Chicago Theatres. Hot Tix sells half-price tickets to many theatrical productions, concerts, and dance performances in Chicago and its environs, provided you are willing to go out and buy them on the day of the show (certain Sunday tickets are available on Saturday). Bring a credit card, check, or cash to a Hot Tix location—on the sixth level of the Chicago Place mall (700 N. Michigan Ave.), across from Marshall Field's in the Loop (108 N. State St.), or at the City Parking Garage in Evanston (1616 Sherman Ave.)—or pay cash only at Lincoln Park's branch of Tower Records (2301 N. Clark St.). Tickets generally don't sell out until late in the day, but as you might guess, your chances of getting into the performance you want are better the earlier you arrive; outlets are open every day. For members, **Hot Tix by Mail** offers 40 to 50 percent discounts by mail, for up to 30 different shows, every eight weeks. For a $10 annual membership, subscribers can order advance tickets to selected shows, through a bimonthly newsletter.

Visitor information... The **Chicago Office of Tourism** (tel 312/744–2400, 800/ITS–CHGO) operates three visitor information centers: the historic **Water Tower**, at Chicago and North Michigan avenues (open until 6pm, 5pm Sundays), the **Chicago Cultural Center**, 77 E. Randolph Street (open until 6pm weekdays, 5pm weekends), and **Illinois Market Place**, a retail shop at Navy Pier (open until 9pm Mon–Thur, 10pm Fri–Sat, 7pm Sun). Or call 800/2CONNECT for a free packet of information on events and attractions in the city. You can also request information from the **Chicago Convention and Tourism Bureau** (tel 312/567–8500).